To Shelley & Dave

Best Wishes

Christmas 1986.

From

Emma & Ian.

POEMS OF
BANJO PATERSON

Illustrated by Pro Hart

THE TRAVELLING POST OFFICE
Oil on hardboard 35 x 45 cm 1976

POEMS OF
BANJO PATERSON

Illustrated by Pro Hart

LANSDOWNE PRESS
Sydney • Auckland • London • New York

Published by Lansdowne Press, Sydney
a division of RPLA Pty Limited
176 South Creek Road, Dee Why West, N.S.W., Australia, 2099.
First published 1982
Second impression 1983
Third impression 1984
Fourth impression 1986
© Text copyright reserved
© Paintings copyright Pro Hart 1974
Produced in Australia by the Publisher
Printed by Kyodo Printing Company, Limited
112 Neythal Road, Jurong Town, Singapore

National Library of Australia Cataloguing-in-Publication Data

Paterson, A.B. (Andrew Barton), 1864-1941.
 Poems by Banjo Paterson.

 Previously published as 2 separate v.: Sydney:
 Ure Smith, 1974 and 1976.
 ISBN 0 7018 1663 5.

 1. Hart, Pro, 1928- . I. Hart, Pro, 1928-
 II. Title

A821'.2

Contents

Prelude

I have gathered these stories afar
  In the wind and the rain,
In the land where the cattle-camps are,
  On the edge of the plain.
On the overland routes of the west,
  When the watches were long,
I have fashioned in earnest and jest
  These fragments of song.

They are just the rude stories one hears
  In sadness and mirth,
The records of wandering years—
  And scant is their worth.
Though their merits indeed are but slight,
  I shall not repine
If they give you one moment's delight,
  Old comrades of mine.

Introduction

As the author of the famous ballads *Clancy of the Overflow, Waltzing Matilda,* and *The Man from Snowy River,* Andrew Barton ('Banjo') Paterson, has become a symbol of the outback for most Australians. But he managed to cram into an eventful life a great deal more than just writing bush ballads. He was also lawyer, grazier, traveller, journalist, editor, war correspondent, soldier, sportsman, and noted horseman.

Paterson was born on 17th February, 1864 at Narambla, near Orange in New South Wales. During his childhood on his father's property he became an expert horseman and many of his later poems commemorate his love of horse-racing and polo.

He was educated at Sydney Grammar, and during his schooldays lived with his grandmother, Emily Barton, at Gladesville. She wrote poetry and exerted a significant influence over the young Paterson. At sixteen he matriculated and was articled to a Sydney law firm.

Paterson began writing and contributing verse to *The Bulletin* during the late 1880s. He used the pseudonym of 'The Banjo', after a racehorse his father had owned, and his work soon became very popular.

He loved the Australian outback, and combined in verse both action itself and the landscape of action. And there is always in all his writings the laconic humour and fatalistic philosophy of the bushman—constantly faced with drought, heat, flies and dust—yet never going under.

Paterson's poetry belongs to the ballad tradition, the folk poetry passed down to us from the Mediaeval bards. He took the ballad genre and moulded it to fit his songs and stories of the Australian bush. His poems capture exactly the spirit and essence of the people, the vast distances and the harsh and beautiful places of outback Australia.

Through many of his ballads he also became one of Australia's greatest myth makers, not least in *Waltzing Matilda.* His jolly swagman, written to the tune of an old English marching song, has become so symbolic of Australia that it is the nearest thing we have to an indigenous national anthem.

Banjo Paterson was a true folk poet—many of his poems are as much a part of the Australian way of life and tradition as steak and eggs, Bondi Beach and beer. In his lifetime he published several books of verse, two novels, a collection of short stories, a book of memoirs, and the first collection of Australian bush songs. But even more than that, he helped form the Australian heritage and gave city people a glimpse of the beauty and legendary magic of the bush.

Clancy
of the
Overflow

I HAD written him a letter which I had, for want of better
    Knowledge, sent to where I met him down the Lachlan years ago;
He was shearing when I knew him, so I sent the letter to him,
    Just on spec, addressed as follows, "Clancy, of The Overflow".

And an answer came directed in a writing unexpected
    (And I think the same was written with a thumb-nail dipped
        in tar);
'Twas his shearing mate who wrote it, and *verbatim* I will quote it:
    "Clancy's gone to Queensland droving, and we don't know where
        he are."

          .   .   .   .   .

In my wild erratic fancy visions come to me of Clancy
    Gone a-droving "down the Cooper" where the Western drovers go;
As the stock are slowly stringing, Clancy rides behind them singing,
    For the drover's life has pleasures that the townsfolk never know.

And the bush has friends to meet him, and their kindly voices
        greet him
    In the murmur of the breezes and the river on its bars,
And he sees the vision splendid of the sunlit plains extended,
    And at night the wondrous glory of the everlasting stars.

          .   .   .   .   .

I am sitting in my dingy little office, where a stingy
    Ray of sunlight struggles feebly down between the houses tall,
And the foetid air and gritty of the dusty, dirty city,
    Through the open window floating, spreads its foulness over all.

And in place of lowing cattle, I can hear the fiendish rattle
    Of the tramways and the buses making hurry down the street;
And the language uninviting of the gutter children fighting
    Comes fitfully and faintly through the ceaseless tramp of feet.

And the hurrying people daunt me, and their pallid faces haunt me
    As they shoulder one another in their rush and nervous haste,
With their eager eyes and greedy, and their stunted forms and
        weedy,
    For townsfolk have no time to grow, they have no time to waste.

And I somehow rather fancy that I'd like to change with Clancy,
    Like to take a turn at droving where the seasons come and go,
While he faced the round eternal of the cash-book and the journal—
    But I doubt he'd suit the office, Clancy, of The Overflow.

CLANCY OF THE OVERFLOW
Oil on canvas board 18in. × 14in. 1974

Geebung Polo Club

It was somewhere up the country, in a land of rock and scrub,
That they formed an institution called the Geebung Polo Club.
They were long and wiry natives from the rugged mountain side,
And the horse was never saddled that the Geebungs couldn't ride;
But their style of playing polo was irregular and rash—
They had mighty little science, but a mighty lot of dash:
And they played on mountain ponies that were muscular and
    strong,
Though their coats were quite unpolished, and their manes and tails
    were long.
And they used to train those ponies wheeling cattle in the scrub;
They were demons, were the members of the Geebung Polo Club.

It was somewhere down the country, in a city's smoke and steam,
That a polo club existed, called "The Cuff and Collar Team".
As a social institution 'twas a marvellous success,
For the members were distinguished by exclusiveness and dress.
They had natty little ponies that were nice, and smooth, and sleek,
For their cultivated owners only rode 'em once a week.
So they started up the country in pursuit of sport and fame,
For they meant to show the Geebungs how they ought to play
    the game;
And they took their valets with them—just to give their boots a rub
Ere they started operations on the Geebung Polo Club.

Now my readers can imagine how the contest ebbed and flowed,
When the Geebung boys got going it was time to clear the road;
And the game was so terrific that ere half the time was gone
A spectator's leg was broken—just from merely looking on.
For they waddied one another till the plain was strewn with dead,
While the score was kept so even that they neither got ahead.
And the Cuff and Collar Captain, when he tumbled off to die
Was the last surviving player—so the game was called a tie.
Then the Captain of the Geebungs raised him slowly from the
    ground,
Though his wounds were mostly mortal, yet he fiercely gazed
    around;
There was no one to oppose him—all the rest were in a trance,
So he scrambled on his pony for his last expiring chance,
For he meant to make an effort to get victory to his side;
So he struck at goal—and missed it—then he tumbled off and died.
    .   .   .   .   .   .

By the old Campaspe River, where the breezes shake the grass,
There's a row of little gravestones that the stockmen never pass,
For they bear a rude inscription saying, "Stranger, drop a tear,
For the Cuff and Collar players and the Geebung boys lie here."
And on misty moonlit evenings, while the dingoes howl around,
You can see their shadows flitting down that phantom polo ground;
You can hear the loud collisions as the flying players meet,
And the rattle of the mallets, and the rush of ponies' feet,
Till the terrified spectator rides like blazes to the pub—
He's been haunted by the spectres of the Geebung Polo Club.

GEEBUNG POLO CLUB
Oil on canvas board 18in. × 14in. 1974

Lost

"HE ought to be home," said the old man. "without there's something amiss.
He only went to the Two-mile—he ought to be back by this.
He *would* ride the Reckless filly, he *would* have his wilful way;
And here, he's not back at sundown—and what will his mother say?

"He was always his mother's idol, since ever his father died;
And there isn't a horse on the station that he isn't game to ride.
But that Reckless mare is vicious, and if once she gets away
He hasn't got strength to hold her—and what will his mother say?"

The old man walked to the sliprail, and peered up the darkening track,
And looked and longed for the rider that would never more come back;
And the mother came and clutched him, with sudden, spasmodic fright:
"What has become of my Willie?—why isn't he home tonight?"

Away in the gloomy ranges, at the foot of an ironbark,
The bonnie, winsome laddie was lying stiff and stark;
For the Reckless mare had smashed him against a leaning limb,
And his comely face was battered, and his merry eyes were dim.

And the thoroughbred chestnut filly, the saddle beneath her flanks,
Was away like fire through the ranges to join the wild mob's ranks;
And a broken-hearted woman and an old man worn and white
Were searching all day in the ranges till the sundown brought the night.

And the mother kept feebly calling, with a hope that would not die,
"Willie! where are you, Willie?" But how can the dead reply?
And hope died out with the daylight, and the darkness brought despair.
God pity the stricken mother, and answer the widow's prayer!

Though far and wide they sought him, they found not where he fell;
For the ranges held him precious, and guarded their treasure well.
The wattle blooms above him, and the blue bells blow close by,
And the brown bees buzz the secret, and the wild birds sing reply.

LOST
Oil on canvas board 18in. × 14in. 1974

But the mother pined and faded, and cried, and took no rest,
And rode each day to the ranges on her hopeless, weary quest,
Seeking her loved one ever, she faded and pined away,
But with strength of her great affection she still sought every day.

"I know that sooner or later I shall find my boy," she said.
But she came not home one evening, and they found her lying dead,
And stamped on the poor pale features, as the spirit homeward
    passed,
Was an angel smile of gladness—she had found her boy at last.

The Man From Snowy River

There was movement at the station, for the word had passed around
  That the colt from old Regret had got away,
And had joined the wild bush horses—he was worth a thousand pound,
  So all the cracks had gathered to the fray.
All the tried and noted riders from the stations near and far
  Had mustered at the homestead overnight,
For the bushmen love hard riding where the wild bush horses are,
  And the stock-horse snuffs the battle with delight.

There was Harrison, who made his pile when Pardon won the cup,
  The old man with his hair as white as snow;
But few could ride beside him when his blood was fairly up—
  He would go wherever horse and man could go.
And Clancy of the Overflow came down to lend a hand,
  No better horseman ever held the reins;
For never horse could throw him while the saddle-girths would stand—
  He learnt to ride while droving on the plains.

And one was there, a stripling on a small and weedy beast;
  He was something like a racehorse undersized,
With a touch of Timor pony—three parts thoroughbred at least—
  And such as are by mountain horsemen prized.
He was hard and tough and wiry—just the sort that won't say die—
  There was courage in his quick impatient tread;
And he bore the badge of gameness in his bright and fiery eye,
  And the proud and lofty carriage of his head.

But still so slight and weedy, one would doubt his power to stay,
  And the old man said, "That horse will never do
For a long and tiring gallop—lad, you'd better stop away,
  Those hills are far too rough for such as you."
So he waited, sad and wistful—only Clancy stood his friend—
  "I think we ought to let him come," he said:
"I warrant he'll be with us when he's wanted at the end,
  For both his horse and he are mountain bred.

"He hails from Snowy River, up by Kosciusko's side,
  Where the hills are twice as steep and twice as rough;
Where a horse's hoofs strike firelight from the flint stones every stride,
  The man that holds his own is good enough.
And the Snowy River riders on the mountains make their home,
  Where the river runs those giant hills between;
I have seen full many horsemen since I first commenced to roam,
But nowhere yet such horsemen have I seen."

So he went; they found the horses by the big mimosa clump,
    They raced. away towards the mountain's brow,
And the old man gave his orders, "Boys, go at them from the jump,
    No use to try for fancy riding now.
And, Clancy, you must wheel them, try and wheel them to the right.
    Ride boldly, lad, and never fear the spills,
For never yet was rider that could keep the mob in sight,
    If once they gain the shelter of those hills."

So Clancy rode to wheel them—he was racing on the wing
    Where the best and boldest riders take their place,
And he raced his stock-horse past them, and he made the ranges ring
    With the stockwhip, as he met them face to face.
Then they halted for a moment, while he swung the dreaded lash,
    But they saw their well-loved mountain full in view,
And they charged beneath the stockwhip with a sharp and sudden
      dash,
    And off into the mountain scrub they flew.

Then fast the horsemen followed, where the gorges deep and black
    Resounded to the thunder of their tread,
And the stockwhips woke the echoes, and they fiercely answered
      back
    From cliffs and crags that beetled overhead.
And upward, ever upward, the wild horses held their way,
    Where mountain ash and kurrajong grew wide;
And the old man muttered fiercely, "We may bid the mob good day,
    No man can hold them down the other side."

When they reached the mountain's summit, even Clancy took a
      pull—
    It well might make the boldest hold their breath;
The wild hop scrub grew thickly, and the hidden ground was full
    Of wombat holes, and any slip was death.

But the man from Snowy River let the pony have his head,
    And he swung his stockwhip round and gave a cheer,
And he raced him down the mountain like a torrent down its bed,
    While the others stood and watched in very fear.

He sent the flint-stones flying, but the pony kept his feet,
    He cleared the fallen timber in his stride,
And the man from Snowy River never shifted in his seat—
    It was grand to see that mountain horseman ride.
Through the stringy barks and saplings, on the rough and broken
      ground,
    Down the hillside at a racing pace he went;
And he never drew the bridle till he landed safe and sound
    At the bottom of that terrible descent.

THE MAN FROM SNOWY RIVER
Oil on canvas board 18in. × 14in. 1974

He was right among the horses as they climbed the farther hill,
  And the watchers on the mountain, standing mute,
Saw him ply the stockwhip fiercely; he was right among them still,
  As he raced across the clearing in pursuit.
Then they lost him for a moment, where two mountain gullies met
  In the ranges—but a final glimpse reveals
On a dim and distant hillside the wild horses racing yet,
  With the man from Snowy River at their heels.

And he ran them single-handed till their sides were white with foam;
  He followed like a bloodhound on their track,
Till they halted, cowed and beaten; then he turned their heads for
    home,
  And alone and unassisted brought them back.
But his hardy mountain pony he could scarcely raise a trot,
  He was blood from hip to shoulder from the spur;
But his pluck was still undaunted, and his courage fiery hot,
  For never yet was mountain horse a cur.

And down by Kosciusko, where the pine-clad ridges raise
  Their torn and rugged battlements on high,
Where the air is clear as crystal, and the white stars fairly blaze
  At midnight in the cold and frosty sky,
And where around the Overflow the reed-beds sweep and sway
  To the breezes, and the rolling plains are wide,
The Man from Snowy River is a household word today,
  And the stockmen tell the story of his ride.

THE MAN FROM SNOWY RIVER
Oil on canvas board 18in. × 14in. 1974

The Swagman's Rest

WE buried old Bob where the bloodwoods wave
   At the foot of the Eaglehawk;
We fashioned a cross on the old man's grave
   For fear that his ghost might walk;
We carved his name on a bloodwood tree
   With the date of his sad decease
And in place of "Died from effects of spree"
   We wrote "May he rest in peace".

For Bob was known on the Overland,
   A regular old bush wag,
Tramping along in the dust and sand,
   Humping his well-worn swag.
He would camp for days in the river-bed,
   And loiter and "fish for whales".
"I'm into the swagman's yard," he said.
   "And I never shall find the rails."

But he found the rails on that summer night
   For a better place—or worse,
As we watched by turns in the flickering light
   With an old black gin for nurse.
The breeze came in with the scent of pine,
   The river sounded clear,
When a change came on, and we saw the sign
   That told us the end was near.

He spoke in a cultured voice and low—
   "I fancy they've 'sent the route';
I once was an army man, you know.
   Though now I'm a drunken brute;
But bury me out where the bloodwoods wave,
   And, if ever you're fairly stuck,
Just take and shovel me out of the grave
   And, maybe, I'll bring you luck.

THE SWAGMAN'S REST
Oil on hardboard 18in. × 14in. 1974

"For I've always heard—" here his voice grew weak,
    His strength was wellnigh sped,
He gasped and struggled and tried to speak,
    Then fell in a moment—dead.
Thus ended a wasted life and hard,
    Of energies misapplied—
Old Bob was out of the "swagman's yard"
    And over the Great Divide.

.   .   .   .   .

The drought came down on the field and flock,
    And never a raindrop fell,
Though the tortured moans of the starving stock
    Might soften a fiend from hell.
And we thought of the hint that the swagman gave
    When he went to the Great Unseen—
We shovelled the skeleton out of the grave
    To see what his hint might mean.

We dug where the cross and the grave posts were,
    We shovelled away the mould,
When sudden a vein of quartz lay bare
    All gleaming with yellow gold.
'Twas a reef with never a fault nor baulk
    That ran from the range's crest,
And the richest mine on the Eaglehawk
    Is known as "The Swagman's Rest".

The Road to Hogan's Gap

Now look, you see, it's this way like—
  You cross the broken bridge
And run the crick down, till you strike
  The second right-hand ridge.

The track is hard to see in parts,
  But still it's pretty clear;
There's been two Injun hawkers' carts
  Along that road this year.

Well, run that right-hand ridge along—
  It ain't, to say, too steep—
There's two fresh tracks might put you wrong
  Where blokes went out with sheep.

But keep the crick upon your right,
  And follow pretty straight
Along the spur, until you sight
  A wire and sapling gate.

Well, that's where Hogan's old grey mare
  Fell off and broke her back;
You'll see her carcass layin' there,
  Jist down below the track.

And then you drop two mile, or three,
  It's pretty steep and blind;
You want to go and fall a tree
  And tie it on behind.

And then you pass a broken cart
  Below a granite bluff;
And that is where you strike the part
  They reckon pretty rough.

But by the time you've got that far
  It's either cure or kill,
So turn your horses round the spur
  And face 'em up the hill.

For look, if you should miss the slope
  And get below the track,
You haven't got the slightest hope
  Of ever gettin' back.

An' half way up you'll see the hide
  Of Hogan's brindled bull;
Well, mind and keep the right-hand side.
  The left's too steep a pull.

And both the banks is full of cracks;
   An' just about at dark
You'll see the last year's bullock tracks
   Where Hogan drew the bark.

The marks is old and pretty faint—
   O'ergrown with scrub and such;
Of course the track to Hogan's ain't
   A road that's travelled much.

But turn and run the tracks along
   For half a mile or more,
And then, of course, you can't go wrong—
   You're right at Hogan's door.

When first you come to Hogan's gate
   He mightn't show perhaps;
He's pretty sure to plant, and wait
   To see it ain't the traps.

I wouldn't call it good enough
   To let your horses out;
There's some that's pretty extra rough
   Is livin' round about.

It's likely, if your horses did
   Get feedin' near the track
It's going to cost at least a quid
   Or more to get them back.

So, if you find they're off the place,
   It's up to you to go
And flash a quid in Hogan's face—
   He'll know the blokes that know.

But listen—if you're feelin' dry,
   Just see there's no one near,
And go and wink the other eye
   And ask for ginger beer.

The blokes come in from near and far
   To sample Hogan's pop;
They reckon once they breast the bar
   They stay there till they drop.

On Sundays you can see them spread
   Like flies around the tap.
It's like that song "The Livin' Dead"
   Up there at Hogan's Gap.

THE ROAD TO HOGAN'S GAP
Oil on hardboard 18in. × 14in. 1974

They like to make it pretty strong
  Whenever there's a chance;
So when a stranger comes along
  They always hold a dance.

There's recitations, songs, and fights—
  A willin' lot you'll meet.
There's one long bloke up there recites;
  I tell you he's a treat.

They're lively blokes all right up there,
  It's never dull a day.
I'd go meself if I could spare
  The time to get away.

      .   .   .   .   .   .

The stranger turned his horses quick.
  He didn't cross the bridge;
He didn't go along the crick
  To strike the second ridge;

He didn't make the trip, because
  He wasn't feeling fit.
His business up at Hogan's was
  To serve him with a writ.

He reckoned, if he faced the pull
  And climbed the rocky stair,
The next to come might find his hide
A landmark on the mountain side,
Along with Hogan's brindled bull
  And Hogan's old grey mare!

THE ROAD TO HOGAN'S GAP
Oil on canvas board 16in. × 13½in. 1974

Song of the Wheat

We have sung the song of the droving days,
  Of the march of the travelling sheep—
How by silent stages and lonely ways
  Thin, white battalions creep.
But the man who now by the land would thrive
  Must his spurs to a ploughshare beat;
And the bush bard, changing his tune, may strive
  To sing the song of the Wheat!

It's west by south of the Great Divide
  The grim grey plains run out,
Where the old flock-masters lived and died
  In a ceaseless fight with drought.
Weary with waiting and hope deferred
  They were ready to own defeat,
Till at last they heard the master-word—
  And the master-word was Wheat.

Yarran and Myall and Box and Pine—
  'Twas axe and fire for all;
They scarce could tarry to blaze the line
  Or wait for the trees to fall
Ere the team was yoked, and the gates flung wide,
  And the dust of the horses' feet
Rose up like a pillar of smoke to guide
  The wonderful march of Wheat.

Furrow by furrow, and fold by fold,
  The soil is turned on the plain;
Better than silver and better than gold
  Is the surface-mine of the grain.
Better than cattle and better than sheep
  In the fight with drought and heat;
For a streak of stubbornness, wide and deep,
  Lies hid in a grain of Wheat.

When the stock is swept by the hand of fate,
  Deep down on his bed of clay
The brave brown Wheat will die and wait
  For the resurrection day—
Lie hid while the whole world thinks him dead;
  But the Spring-rain, soft and sweet,
Will over the steaming paddocks spread
  The first green flush of the Wheat.

SONG OF THE WHEAT
Oil on hardboard 18in. × 14in. 1974

Green and amber and gold it grows
  When the sun sinks late in the West;
And the breeze sweeps over the rippling rows
  Where the quail and the skylark nest.
Mountain or river or shining star,
  There's never a sight can beat—
Away to the sky-line stretching far—
  A sea of the ripening Wheat.

When the burning harvest sun sinks low,
  And shadows stretch on the plain,
The roaring strippers come and go
  Like ships on a sea of grain.
Till the lurching, groaning waggons bear
  Their tale of the load complete.
Of the world's great work he has done his share
  Who has garnered a crop of wheat.

Princes, Potentates, Kings and Czars,
  They travel in regal state,
But old King Wheat has a thousand cars
  For his trip to the water-gate;
And his thousand steamships breast the tide
  And plough through the wind and sleet
To the lands where the teeming millions bide
  That say: "Thank God for Wheat!"

Mulga Bill's Bicycle

'Twas Mulga Bill, from Eaglehawk, that caught the cycling craze;
He turned away the good old horse that served him many days;
He dressed himself in cycling clothes, resplendent to be seen;
He hurried off to town and bought a shining new machine;
And as he wheeled it through the door, with air of lordly pride,
The grinning shop assistant said, "Excuse me, can you ride?"

"See here, young man," said Mulga Bill, "from Walgett to the sea,
From Conroy's Gap to Castlereagh, there's none can ride like me.
I'm good all round at everything, as everybody knows,
Although I'm not the one to talk—I hate a man that blows.

"But riding is my special gift, my chiefest, sole delight;
Just ask a wild duck can it swim, a wild cat can it fight.
There's nothing clothed in hair or hide, or built of flesh or steel,
There's nothing walks or jumps, or runs, on axle, hoof, or wheel,
But what I'll sit, while hide will hold and girths and straps are tight;
I'll ride this here two-wheeled concern right straight away at sight."

'Twas Mulga Bill, from Eaglehawk, that sought his own abode,
That perched above the Dead Man's Creek, beside the mountain
    road.
He turned the cycle down the hill and mounted for the fray,
But ere he'd gone a dozen yards it bolted clean away.
It left the track, and through the trees, just like a silver streak,
It whistled down the awful slope towards the Dead Man's Creek.

It shaved a stump by half an inch, it dodged a big white-box:
The very wallaroos in fright went scrambling up the rocks,
The wombats hiding in their caves dug deeper underground,
But Mulga Bill, as white as chalk, sat tight to every bound.
It struck a stone and gave a spring that cleared a fallen tree,
It raced beside a precipice as close as close could be;
And then, as Mulga Bill let out one last despairing shriek,
It made a leap of twenty feet into the Dead Man's Creek.

'Twas Mulga Bill, from Eaglehawk, that slowly swam ashore:
He said, "I've had some narrer shaves and lively rides before;
I've rode a wild bull round a yard to win a five-pound bet,
But this was sure the derndest ride that I've encountered yet.
I'll give that two-wheeled outlaw best; it's shaken all my nerve
To feel it whistle through the air and plunge and buck, and swerve,
It's safe at rest in Dead Man's Creek—we'll leave it lying still;
A horse's back is good enough henceforth for Mulga Bill."

MULGA BILL'S BICYCLE
Oil on canvas board 18in. × 14in. 1974

Waltzing Matilda

(*Carrying a Swag*)

OH! there once was a swagman camped in a Billabong,
    Under the shade of a Coolabah tree;
And he sang as he looked at his old billy boiling,
    "Who'll come a-waltzing Matilda with me?"

    Who'll come a-waltzing Matilda, my darling,
        Who'll come a-waltzing Matilda with me?
    Waltzing Matilda and leading a water-bag—
        Who'll come a-waltzing Matilda with me?

Down came a jumbuck to drink at the water-hole,
    Up jumped the swagman and grabbed him in glee;
And he sang as he stowed him away in his tucker-bag,
    "You'll come a-waltzing Matilda with me."

Down came the Squatter a-riding his thoroughbred;
    Down came Policemen—one, two and three.
      "Whose is the jumbuck you've got in the tucker-bag?
    You'll come a-waltzing Matilda with me."

But the swagman, he up and he jumped in the water-hole,
    Drowning himself by the Coolabah tree;
And his ghost may be heard as it sings in the Billabong
    "Who'll come a-waltzing Matilda with me?"

"SWAGMAN WITH SHEEP"

WALTZING MATILDA
Oil on hardboard 18in. × 14in. 1974

Saltbush Bill

Now this is the law of the Overland that all in the West obey—
A man must cover with travelling sheep a six-mile stage a day;
But this is the law which the drovers make, right easily understood,
They travel their stage where the grass is bad, but they camp
  where the grass is good;
They camp, and they ravage the squatter's grass till never a
  blade remains.
Then they drift away as the white clouds drift on the edge of the
  saltbush plains:
From camp to camp and from run to run they battle it hand to
  hand
For a blade of grass and the right to pass on the track of the
  Overland.
For this is the law of the Great Stock Routes, 'tis written in
  white and black—
The man that goes with a travelling mob must keep to a half-mile
  track;
And the drovers keep to a half-mile track on the runs where the
  grass is dead,
But they spread their sheep on a well-grassed run till they go
  with a two-mile spread.
So the squatters hurry the drovers on from dawn till the fall of
  night,
And the squatters' dogs and the drovers' dogs get mixed in a
  deadly fight.
Yet the squatters' men, though they haunt the mob, are willing
  the peace to keep,
For the drovers learn how to use their hands when they go with
  the travelling sheep;
But this is the tale of a Jackeroo that came from a foreign strand,
And the fight that he fought with Saltbush Bill, the King of
  the Overland.

Now Saltbush Bill was a drover tough as ever the country knew,
He had fought his way on the Great Stock Routes from the sea
  to the big Barcoo;
He could tell when he came to a friendly run that gave him a
  chance to spread,
And he knew where the hungry owners were that hurried his
  sheep ahead;
He was drifting down in the Eighty drought with a mob that
  could scarcely creep
(When the kangaroos by the thousand starve, it is rough on the
  travelling sheep),

SALTBUSH BILL
Oil on canvas board 18in. × 14in. 1974

And he camped one night at the crossing-place on the edge of
the Wilga run;
"We must manage a feed for them here," he said, "or half of the
mob are done!"
So he spread them out when they left the camp wherever they
liked to go,
Till he grew aware of a Jackeroo with a station-hand in tow.
They set to work on the straggling sheep, and with many a stock-
whip crack
They forced them in where the grass was dead in the space of
the half-mile track;
And William prayed that the hand of Fate might suddenly strike
him blue
But he'd get some grass for his starving sheep in the teeth of that
Jackeroo.
So he turned and he cursed the Jackeroo; he cursed him, alive
or dead,
From the soles of his great unwieldly feet to the crown of his
ugly head,
With an extra curse on the moke he rode and the cur at his heels
that ran,
Till the Jackaroo from his horse got down and went for the drover-
man;
With the station-hand for his picker-up, though the sheep ran
loose the while,
They battled it out on the well-grassed plain in the regular prize-
ring style.

Now, the new chum fought for his honour's sake and the pride
of the English race,
But the drover fought for his daily bread with a smile on his
bearded face;
So he shifted ground, and he sparred for wind, and he made it
a lengthy mill,
And from time to time as his scouts came in they whispered to
Saltbush Bill—
"We have spread the sheep with a two-mile spread, and the grass
it is something grand;
You must stick to him, Bill, for another round for the pride of
the Overland."

The new chum made it a rushing fight, though never a blow
    got home,
Till the sun rode high in the cloudless sky and glared on the
    brick-red loam,
Till the sheep drew in to the shelter-trees and settled them down
    to rest;
Then the drover said he would fight no more, and gave his
    opponent best.

So the new chum rode to the homestead straight, and told them a
    story grand
Of the desperate fight that he fought that day with the King
    of the Overland;
And the tale went home to the Public Schools of the pluck of the
    English swell—
How the drover fought for his very life, but blood in the end
    must tell.
But the travelling sheep and the Wilga sheep were boxed on the
    Old Man Plain;
'Twas a full week's work ere they drafted out and hunted them
    off again;
A week's good grass in their wretched hides, with a curse and a
    stockwhip crack
They hunted them off on the road once more to starve on the
    half-mile track.
And Saltbush Bill, on the Overland, will many a time recite
How the best day's work that he ever did was the day that he
    lost the fight.

In Defence of the Bush

So you're back from up the country, Mister Lawson, where you
    went,
And you're cursing all the business in a bitter discontent;
Well, we grieve to disappoint you, and it makes us sad to hear
That it wasn't cool and shady—and there wasn't whips of beer,
And the looney bullock snorted when you first came into view—
Well, you know it's not so often that he sees a swell like you;
And the roads were hot and dusty, and the plains were burnt
    and brown,
And no doubt you're better suited drinking lemon-squash in town.
Yet, perchance, if you should journey down the very track you
    went
In a month or two at furthest, you would wonder what it meant;
Where the sunbaked earth was gasping like a creature in its pain
You would find the grasses waving like a field of summer grain,
And the miles of thirsty gutters, blocked with sand and choked
    with mud,
You would find them mighty rivers with a turbid, sweeping flood.
For the rain and drought and sunshine make no changes in the
    street,
In the sullen line of buildings and the ceaseless tramp of feet;
But the bush has moods and changes, as the seasons rise and fall,
And the men who know the bush-land—they are loyal through it all.

       .   .   .   .   .   .

But you found the bush was dismal and a land of no delight—
Did you chance to hear a chorus in the shearers' huts at night?
Did they "rise up William Riley" by the camp-fire's cheery blaze?
Did they rise him as we rose him in the good old droving days?
And the women of the homesteads and the men you chanced to
    meet—
Were their faces sour and saddened like the "faces in the street"?
And the "shy selector children"—were they better now or worse
Than the little city urchins who would greet you with a curse?
Is not such a life much better than the squalid street and square
Where the fallen women flaunt it in the fierce electric glare,
Where the sempstress plies her needle till her eyes are sore and red
In a filthy, dirty attic toiling on for daily bread?

IN DEFENCE OF THE BUSH
Oil on canvas board 18in. × 14in. 1974

Did you hear no sweeter voices in the music of the bush
Than the roar of trams and buses, and the war-whoop of "the push"?
Did the magpies rouse your slumbers with their carol sweet and
strange?
Did you hear the silver chiming of the bell-birds on the range?
But, perchance, the wild birds' music by your senses was despised,
For you say you'll stay in townships till the bush is civilized.
Would you make it a tea-garden, and on Sundays have a band
Where the "blokes" might take their "donahs", with a "public"
close at hand?
You had better stick to Sydney and make merry with the "push",
For the bush will never suit you, and you'll never suit the bush.

When Dacey Rode the Mule

'TWAS to a small, up-country town,
  When we were boys at school,
There came a circus with a clown,
  Likewise a bucking mule.
The clown announced a scheme they had
  Spectators for to bring—
They'd give a crown to any lad
  Who'd ride him round the ring.

And, gentle reader, do not scoff
  Nor think a man a fool—
To buck a porous-plaster off
  Was pastime to that mule.

The boys got on he bucked like sin;
  He threw them in the dirt.
What time the clown wouid raise a grin
  By asking, "Are you hurt?"
But Johnny Dacey came one night,
  The crack of all the school;
Said he, "I'll win the crown all right;
  Bring in your bucking mule."

The elephant went off his trunk,
  The monkey played the fool,
And all the band got blazing drunk
  When Dacey rode the mule.

But soon there rose a galling shout
  Of laughter, for the clown
From somewhere in his pants drew out
  A little paper crown.
He placed the crown on Dacey's head
  While Dacey looked a fool;
"Now, there's your crown, my lad," he said,
  "For riding of the mule!"

The band struck up with "Killaloe",
  And "Rule Britannia, Rule",
And "Young Man from the Country", too,
  When Dacey rode the mule.
Then Dacey, in a furious rage,
  For vengeance on the show
Ascended to the monkeys' cage
  And let the monkeys go;
The blue-tailed ape and the chimpanzee
  He turned abroad to roam;
Good faith! It was a sight to see
  The people step for home.

For big baboons with canine snout
Are spiteful, as a rule—
The people didn't sit it out,
When Dacey rode the mule.

And from the beasts he let escape,
The bushmen all declare,
Were·born some creatures partly ape
And partly native-bear.
They're rather few and far between,
The race is nearly spent;
But some of them may still be seen
In Sydney Parliament.

And when those legislators fight,
And drink, and act the fool,
Just blame it on that torrid night
When Dacey rode the mule.

WHEN DACEY RODE THE MULE
Oil on canvas board 18in. × 14in. 1974

Shearing at Castlereagh

THE bell is set a-ringing, and the engine gives a toot,
There's five-and-thirty shearers here a-shearing for the loot,
So stir yourselves, you penners-up, and shove the sheep along—
The musterers are fetching them a hundred thousand strong—
And make your collie dogs speak up; what would the buyers say
In London if the wool was late this year from Castlereagh?

The man that "rung" the Tubbo shed is not the ringer here,
That stripling from the Cooma-side can teach him how to shear.
They trim away the ragged locks, and rip the cutter goes,
And leaves a track of snowy fleece from brisket to the nose;
It's lovely how they peel it off with never stop nor stay,
They're racing for the ringer's place this year at Castlereagh.

The man that keeps the cutters sharp is growling in his cage,
He's always in a hurry; and he's always in a rage—
"You clumsy-fisted mutton-heads, you'd turn a fellow sick,
You pass yourselves as shearers, you were born to swing a pick.
Another broken cutter here, that's two you've broke today,
It's lovely how they peel it off with never stop nor stay,

The youngsters picking up the fleece enjoy the merry din,
They throw the classer up the fleece, he throws it to the bin;
The pressers standing by the rack are waiting for the wool,
There's room for just a couple more, the press is nearly full;
Now jump upon the lever, lads, and heave and heave away,
Another bale of golden fleece is branded "Castlereagh".

SHEARING AT CASTLEREAGH
Oil on canvas board 18in. × 14in. 1974

The First Surveyor

"THE opening of the railway line!—the Governor and all!
With flags and banners down the street, a banquet and a ball.
Hark to 'em at the station now! They're raising cheer on cheer!
'The man who brought the railway through—our friend the
    engineer.'

"They cheer *his* pluck and enterprise and engineering skill!
'Twas my old husband found the pass behind that big red hill.
Before the engineer was born we'd settled with our stock
Behind that great big mountain chain, a line of range and rock—
A line that kept us starving there in weary weeks of drought,
With ne'er a track across the range to let the cattle out.

" 'Twas then, with horses starved and weak and scarcely fit to crawl,
My husband went to find a way across the rocky wall.
He vanished in the wilderness—God knows where he was gone—
He hunted till his food gave out, but still he battled on.
His horses strayed ('twas well they did), they made towards the
    grass,
And down behind that big red hill they found an easy pass.

"He followed up and blazed the trees, to show the safest track,
Then drew his belt another hole and turned and started back.
His horses died—just one pulled through with nothing much to
    spare;
God bless the beast that brought him home, the old white Arab
    mare!
We drove the cattle through the hills, along the new-found way,
And this was our first camping-ground—just where I live today.

"Then others came across the range and built the township here,
And then there came the railway line and this young engineer;
He drove about with tents and traps, a cook to cook his meals,
A bath to wash himself at night, a chain-man at his heels.
And that was all the pluck and skill for which he's cheered and
    praised,
For after all he took the track, the same my husband blazed!

"My poor old husband, dead and gone with never feast nor cheer;
He's buried by the railway line!—I wonder can he hear
When by the very track he marked, and close to where he's laid,
The cattle trains go roaring down the one-in-thirty grade.
I wonder does he hear them pass, and can he see the sight
When, whistling shrill, the fast express goes flaming by at night.

THE FIRST SURVEYOR
Oil on canvas board 18in. × 14in. 1974

"I think 'twould comfort him to know there's someone left to care;
I'll take some things this very night and hold a banquet there—
The hard old fare we've often shared together, him and me,
Some damper and a bite of beef, a pannikin of tea:
We'll do without the bands and flags, the speeches and the fuss,
We know who *ought* to get the cheers—and that's enough for us.

"What's that? They wish that I'd come down—the oldest settler
    here!
Present me to the Governor and that young engineer!
Well, just you tell his Excellence, and put the thing polite,
I'm sorry, but I can't come down—I'm dining out tonight!"

How Gilbert Died

THERE'S never a stone at the sleeper's head,
　　There's never a fence beside,
And the wandering stock on the grave may tread
　　Unnoticed and undenied;
But the smallest child on the Watershed
　　Can tell you how Gilbert died.

For he rode at dusk with his comrade Dunn
　　To the hut at the Stockman's Ford;
In the waning light of the sinking sun
　　They peered with a fierce accord.
They were outlaws both—and on each man's head
　　Was a thousand pounds reward.

They had taken toll of the country round,
　　And the troopers came behind
With a black who tracked like a human hound
　　In the scrub and the ranges blind:
He could run the trail where a white man's eye
　　No sign of track could find.

He had hunted them out of the One Tree Hill
　　And over the Old Man Plain,
But they wheeled their tracks with a wild beast's skill,
　　And they made for the range again;
Then away to the hut where their grandsire dwelt
　　They rode with a loosened rein.

And their grandsire gave them a greeting bold:
　　"Come in and rest in peace,
No safer place does the country hold—
　　With the night pursuit must cease,
And we'll drink success to the roving boys,
　　And to hell with the black police."

But they went to death when they entered there
　　In the hut at the Stockman's Ford,
For their grandsire's words were as false as fair—
　　They were doomed to the hangman's cord.
He had sold them both to the black police
　　For the sake of the big reward.

In the depth of night there are forms that glide
　　As stealthily as serpents creep,
And around the hut where the outlaws hide
　　They plant in the shadows deep,
And they wait till the first faint flush of dawn
　　Shall waken their prey from sleep.

But Gilbert wakes while the night is dark—
    A restless sleeper aye.
He has heard the sound of a sheep-dog's bark,
    And his horse's warning neigh,
And he says to his mate, "There are hawks abroad,
    And it's time that we went away."

Their rifles stood at the stretcher head,
    Their bridles lay to hand;
They wakened the old man out of his bed,
    When they heard the sharp command:
"In the name of the Queen lay down your arms,
    Now, Dunn and Gilbert, stand!"

Then Gilbert reached for his rifle true
    That close at hand he kept;
He pointed straight at the voice, and drew,
    But never a flash outleapt,
For the water ran from the rifle breech—
    It was drenched while the outlaws slept.

Then he dropped the piece with a bitter oath,
    And he turned to his comrade Dunn:
"We are sold," he said, "we are dead men both!—
    Still, there may be a chance for one;
I'll stop and I'll fight with the pistol here,
    You take to your heels and run."

So Dunn crept out on his hands and knees
    In the dim, half-dawning light,
And he made his way to a patch of trees,
    And was lost in the black of night;
And the trackers hunted his tracks all day,
    But they never could trace his flight.

But Gilbert walked from the open door
    In a confident style and rash;
He heard at his side the rifles roar,
    And he heard the bullets crash.
But he laughed as he lifted his pistol-hand,
    And he fired at the rifle flash.

Then out of the shadows the troopers aimed
    At his voice and the pistol sound.
With rifle flashes the darkness flamed—
    He staggered and spun around,
And they riddled his body with rifle balls
    As it lay on the blood-soaked ground.

HOW GILBERT DIED
Oil on canvas board 18in. × 14in. 1974

There's never a stone at the sleeper's head,
  There's never a fence beside,
And the wandering stock on the grave may tread
  Unnoticed and undenied;
But the smallest child on the Watershed
  Can tell you how Gilbert died.

The Man From Ironbark

It was the man from Ironbark who struck the Sydney town,
He wandered over street and park, he wandered up and down.
He loitered here, he loitered there, till he was like to drop,
Until at last in sheer despair he sought a barber's shop.
" 'Ere! shave my beard and whiskers off, I'll be a man of mark,
I'll go and do the Sydney toff up home in Ironbark."

The barber man was small and flash, as barbers mostly are,
He wore a strike-your-fancy sash, he smoked a huge cigar:
He was a humorist of note and keen at repartee,
He laid the odds and kept a "tote", whatever that may be.
And when he saw our friend arrive, he whispered "Here's a lark!
Just watch me catch him all alive this man from Ironbark."

There were some gilded youths that sat along the barber's wall,
Their eyes were dull, their heads were flat, they had no brains
　　　　at all;
To them the barber passed the wink, his dexter eyelid shut,
"I'll make this bloomin' yokel think his bloomin' throat is cut."
And as he soaped and rubbed it in he made a rude remark:
"I s'pose the flats is pretty green up there in Ironbark."

A grunt was all reply he got; he shaved the bushman's chin,
Then made the water boiling hot and dipped the razor in.
He raised his hand, his brow grew black, he paused awhile to
　　　　gloat,
Then slashed the red-hot razor-back across his victim's throat;
Upon the newly-shaven skin it made a livid mark—
No doubt it fairly took him in—the man from Ironbark.

He fetched a wild up-country yell might wake the dead to hear,
And though his throat, he knew full well, was cut from ear to ear,
He struggled gamely to his feet, and faced the murderous foe.
"You've done for me! you dog, I'm beat! one hit before I go!
I only wish I had a knife, you blessed murdering shark!
But you'll remember all your life the man from Ironbark."

He lifted up his hairy paw, with one tremendous clout
He landed on the barber's jaw, and knocked the barber out.
He set to work with tooth and nail, he made the place a wreck;
He grabbed the nearest gilded youth, and tried to break his neck.
And all the while his throat he held to save his vital spark,
And "Murder! Bloody Murder!" yelled the man from Ironbark.

A peeler man who heard the din came in to see the show;
He tried to run the bushman in, but he refused to go.
And when at last the barber spoke, and said " 'Twas all in fun—
'Twas just a little harmless joke, a trifle overdone."
"A joke!" he cried, "By George, that's fine; a lively sort of lark;
I'd like to catch that murdering swine some night in Ironbark."

And now while round the shearing-floor the listening shearers gape,
He tells the story o'er and o'er and brags of his escape.
"Them barber chaps what keeps a tote, by George, I've had enough,
One tried to cut my bloomin' throat, but thank the Lord it's tough."
And whether he's believed or no, there's one thing to remark,
That flowing beards are all the go way up in Ironbark.

THE MAN FROM IRONBARK
Oil on hardboard 18in. × 14in. 1974

A Bush Christening

On the outer Barcoo where the churches are few,
  And men of religion are scanty,
On a road never cross'd 'cept by folk that are lost
  One Michael Magee had a shanty.

Now this Mike was the dad of a ten-year-old lad,
  Plump, healthy, and stoutly conditioned;
He was strong as the best, but poor Mike had no rest
  For the youngster had never been christened.

And his wife used to cry, "If the darlin' should die
  Saint Peter would not recognize him."
But by luck he survived till a preacher arrived,
  Who agreed straightaway to baptize him.

Now the artful young rogue, while they held their collogue,
  With his ear to the keyhole was listenin';
And he muttered in fright, while his features turned white,
  "What the devil and all is this christenin'?"

He was none of your dolts—he had seen them brand colts.
  And it seemed to his small understanding,
If the man in the frock made him one of the flock,
  It must mean something very like branding.

So away with a rush he set off for the bush,
  While the tears in his eyelids they glistened—
" 'Tis outrageous," says he, "to brand youngsters like me;
  I'll be dashed if I'll stop to be christened!"

Like a young native dog he ran into a log,
  And his father with language uncivil,
Never heeding the "praste", cried aloud in his haste
  "Come out and be christened, you divil!"

But he lay there as snug as a bug in a rug,
  And his parents in vain might reprove him,
Till his reverence spoke (he was fond of a joke)
  "I've a notion," says he, "that'll move him."

"Poke a stick up the log, give the spalpeen a prog;
  Poke him aisy—don't hurt him or maim him;
'Tis not long that he'll stand, I've the water at hand,
  As he rushes out this end I'll name him."

"Here he comes, and for shame! ye've forgotten the name—
  Is it Patsy or Michael or Dinnis?"
Here the youngster ran out, and the priest gave a shout—
  "Take your chance, anyhow, wid 'Maginnis!' "

A BUSH CHRISTENING
Oil on harboard 18in. × 24in. 1974

As the howling young cub ran away to the scrub
    Where he knew that pursuit would be risky,
The priest, as he fled, flung a flask at his head
    That was labelled "Maginnis's Whisky"!

Now Maginnis Magee has been made a J.P.,
    And the one thing he hates more than sin is
To be asked by the folk, who have heard of the joke,
    How he came to be christened Maginnis!

In the Droving Days

"ONLY a pound," said the auctioneer,
"Only a pound; and I'm standing here
Selling this animal, gain or loss—
Only a pound for the drover's horse?
One of the sort that was ne'er afraid,
One of the boys of the Old Brigade;
Thoroughly honest and game, I'll swear,
Only a little the worse for wear;
Plenty as bad to be seen in town,
Give me a bid and I'll knock him down;
Sold as he stands, and without recourse,
Give me a bid for the drover's horse."

Loitering there in an aimless way
Somehow I noticed the poor old grey,
Weary and battered and screwed, of course;
Yet when I noticed the old grey horse,
The rough bush saddle, and single rein
Of the bridle laid on his tangled mane,
Straightway the crowd and the auctioneer
Seemed on a sudden to disappear,
Melted away in a kind of haze—
For my heart went back to the droving days.

Back to the road, and I crossed again
Over the miles of the saltbush plain—
The shining plain that is said to be
The dried-up bed of an inland sea.
Where the air so dry and so clear and bright
Refracts the sun with a wondrous light,
And out in the dim horizon makes
The deep blue gleam of the phantom lakes.

At dawn of day we could feel the breeze
That stirred the boughs of the sleeping trees,
And brought a breath of the fragrance rare
That comes and goes in that scented air;
For the trees and grass and the shrubs contain
A dry sweet scent on the saltbush plain.
For those that love it and understand
The saltbush plain is a wonderland,
A wondrous country, where Nature's ways
Were revealed to me in the droving days.

We saw the fleet wild horses pass,
And kangaroos through the Mitchell grass;
The emu ran with her frightened brood
All unmolested and unpursued.
But there rose a shout and a wild hubbub
When the dingo raced for his native scrub,
And he paid right dear for his stolen meals
With the drovers' dogs at his wretched heels.
For we ran him down at a rattling pace,
While the pack-horse joined in the stirring chase.
And a wild halloo at the kill we'd raise—
We were light of heart in the droving days.

'Twas a drover's horse, and my hand again
Made a move to close on a fancied rein.
For I felt the swing and the easy stride
Of the grand old horse that I used to ride.
In drought or plenty, in good or ill,
The same old steed was my comrade still;
The old grey horse with his honest ways
Was a mate to me in the droving days.

When we kept our watch in the cold and damp,
If the cattle broke from the sleeping camp,
Over the flats and across the plain,
With my head bent down on his waving mane,
Through the boughs above and the stumps below,
On the darkest night I could let him go
At a racing speed; he would choose his course,
And my life was safe with the old grey horse.
But man and horse had a favourite job,
When an outlaw broke from a station mob;
With a right good will was the stockwhip plied,
As the old horse raced at the straggler's side,
And the greenhide whip such a weal would raise—
We could use the whip in the droving days.

. . . . .

"Only a pound!" and was this the end—
Only a pound for the drover's friend.
The drover's friend that has seen his day,
And now was worthless and cast away
With a broken knee and a broken heart
To be flogged and starved in a hawker's cart.
Well, I made a bid for a sense of shame.
And the memories dear of the good old game.

IN THE DROVING DAYS
Oil on canvas board 18in. × 14in. 1974

"Thank you? Guinea! and cheap at that!
Against you there in the curly hat!
Only a guinea, and one more chance,
Down he goes if there's no advance,
Third, and last time, one! two! three!"
And the old grey horse was knocked down to me.
And now he's wandering, fat and sleek,
On the lucerne flats by the Homestead Creek;
I dare not ride him for fear he'd fall,
But he does a journey to beat them all,
For though he scarcely a trot can raise,
He can take me back to the droving days.

Song of the Artesian Water

Now the stock have started dying, for the Lord has sent a drought;
But we're sick of prayers and Providence—we're going to do without;
With the derricks up above us and the solid earth below,
We are waiting at the lever for the word to let her go.
    Sinking down, deeper down
    Oh, we'll sink it deeper down:
As the drill is plugging downward at a thousand feet of level,
If the Lord won't send us water, oh, we'll get it from the devil;
Yes, we'll get it from the devil deeper down.

Now, our engine's built in Glasgow by a very canny Scot,
And he marked it twenty horse-power, but he don't know what is
   what:
When Canadian Bill is firing with the sun-dried gidgee logs,
She can equal thirty horses and a score or so of dogs.
    Sinking down, deeper down,
    Oh, we're going deeper down:
If we fail to get the water, then it's ruin to the squatter,
For the drought is on the station and the weather's growing hotter,
But we're bound to get the water deeper down.

But the shaft has started caving and the sinking's very slow,
And the yellow rods are bending in the water down below,
And the tubes are always jamming and they can't be made to shift
Till we nearly burst the engine with a forty horse-power lift.
    Sinking down, deeper down,
    Oh, we're going deeper down:
Though the shaft is always caving, and the tubes are always jamming,
Yet we'll fight our way to water while the stubborn drill is ramming—
While the stubborn drill is ramming deeper down.

But there's no artesian water, though we've passed three thousand
   feet,
And the contract price is growing, and the boss is nearly beat.
But it must be down beneath us, and it's down we've got to go,
Though she's bumping on the solid rock four thousand feet below.
    Sinking down, deeper down,
    Oh, we're going deeper down:
And it's time they heard us knocking on the roof of Satan's dwellin';
But we'll get artesian water if we cave the roof of hell in—
Oh! we'll get artesian water deeper down.

But it's hark! the whistle's blowing with a wild, exultant blast,
And the boys are madly cheering, for they've struck the flow at
    last;
And it's rushing up the tubing from four thousand feet below,
Till it spouts above the casing in a million-gallon flow.
            And it's down, deeper down—
           Oh, it comes from deeper down;
It is flowing, ever flowing, in a free, unstinted measure
From the silent hidden places where the old earth hides her treasure—
Where the old earth hides her treasures deeper down.

And it's clear away the timber, and it's let the water run;
How it glimmers in the shadow, how it flashes in the sun!
By the silent belts of timber, by the miles of blazing plain
It is bringing hope and comfort to the thirsty land again.
           Flowing down, further down;
           It is flowing further down
To the tortured thirsty cattle, bringing gladness in its going;
Through the droughty days of summer it is flowing, ever flowing—
It is flowing, ever flowing, further down.

SONG OF THE ARTESIAN WATER
Oil on canvas board 18in. × 14in. 1974

Johnson's Antidote

DOWN along the Snakebite River where the overlanders camp,
Where the serpents are in millions, all of the most deadly stamp;
Where the station-cook in terror, nearly every time he bakes,
Mixes up among the doughboys half a dozen poison-snakes;
Where the wily free-selector walks in armour-plated pants,
And defies the stings of scorpions, and the bites of bull-dog ants:
Where the adder and the viper tear each other by the throat—
There it was that William Johnson sought his snake-bite antidote.

Johnson was a free-selector, and his brain went rather queer,
For the constant sight of serpents filled him with a deadly fear;
So he tramped his free-selection, morning, afternoon, and night,
Seeking for some great specific that would cure the serpent's bite
Till King Billy, of the Mooki, chieftain of the flour-bag head,
Told him, "Spos'n snake bite pfeller, pfellar mostly drop down dead;
Spos'n snake bite old goanna, then you watch a while you see
Old goanna cure himself with eating little pfeller tree."
"That's the cure," said William Johnson, "point me out this plant
    sublime."
But King Billy, feeling lazy, said he'd go another time.
Thus it came to pass that Johnson, having got the tale by rote,
Followed every stray goanna seeking for the antidote.

      ·   ·   ·   ·   ·   ·   ·

Loafing once beside the river, while he thought his heart would
    break,
There he saw a big goanna fight with a tiger-snake.
In and out they rolled and wriggled, bit each other, heart and soul,
Till the valiant old goanna swallowed his opponent whole.
Breathless, Johnson sat and watched him, saw him struggle up the
    bank,
Saw him nibbling at the branches of some bushes, green and rank;
Saw him, happy and contented, lick his lips, as off he crept,
While the bulging of his stomach showed where his opponent slept
Then a cheer of exultation burst aloud from Johnson's throat;
"Luck at last," said he, "I've struck it! 'tis the famous antidote.

JOHNSON'S ANTIDOTE
Oil on canvas board 18in. × 14in. 1974

"Here it is, the Grand Elixir, greatest blessing ever known—
Twenty thousand men in India die each year of snakes alone;
Think of all the foreign nations, negro, chow, and blackamoor,
Saved from sudden expiration by my wondrous snakebite cure.
It will bring me fame and fortune! In the happy days to be
Men of every clime and nation will be round to gaze on me—
Scientific men in thousands, men of mark and men of note,
Rushing down the Mooki River, after Johnson's antidote.
It will cure *delirium tremens* when the patient's eyeballs stare
At imaginary spiders, snakes which really are not there.
When he thinks he sees them wriggle, when he thinks he sees them
    bloat,
It will cure him just to think of Johnson's Snakebite Antidote."

Then he rushed to the museum, found a scientific man—
"Trot me out a deadly serpent, just the deadliest you can;
I intend to let him bite me, all the risk I will endure.
Just to prove the sterling value of my wondrous snakebite cure.
Even though an adder bit me, back to life again I'd float;
Snakes are out of date, I tell you, since I've found the antidote."
Said the scientific person, "If you really want to die,
Go ahead—but, if you're doubtful, let your sheep-dog have a try.
Get a pair of dogs and try it, let the snake give both a nip;
Give your dog the snakebite mixture, let the other fellow rip;
If he dies and yours survives him then it proves the thing is good.
Will you fetch your dog and try it?" Johnson rather thought he
    would.
So he went and fetched his canine, hauled him forward by the throat.
"Stump, old man," says he, "we'll show them we've the genwine
    antidote."

JOHNSON'S ANTIDOTE
Oil on canvas board 16in. × 14in. 1974

Both the dogs were duly loaded with the poison-gland's contents;
Johnson gave his dog the mixture, then sat down to wait events.
"Mark," he said, "in twenty minutes Stump'll be a-rushing round,
While the other wretched creature lies a corpse upon the ground."
But, alas for William Johnson! ere they'd watched a half-hour's spell
Stumpy was as dead as mutton, t'other dog was live and well.
And the scientific person hurried off with utmost speed,
Tested Johnson's drug and found it was a deadly poison-weed;
Half a tumbler killed an emu, half a spoonful killed a goat—
All the snakes on earth were harmless to that awful antidote.
Down along the Mooki River, on the overlanders' camp,
Where the serpents are in millions, all of the most deadly stamp,
Wanders, daily, William Johnson, down among those poisonous
    hordes,
Shooting every stray goanna calls them "black and yaller frauds".
And King Billy, of the Mooki, cadging for the cast-off coat,
Somehow seems to dodge the subject of the snakebite antidote.

Only a Jockey

"Richard Bennison, a jockey, aged fourteen, while riding William Tell in his training, was thrown and killed. The horse is luckily uninjured."—Melbourne Wire.

OUT in the grey cheerless chill of the morning light,
    Out on the track where the night shades still lurk,
Ere the first gleam of the sungod's returning light
    Round come the racehorses early at work.

Reefing and pulling and racing so readily,
    Close sit the jockey-boys holding them hard,
"Steady the stallion there—canter him steadily,
    Don't let him gallop so much as a yard."

Fiercely he fights while the others run wide of him,
    Reefs at the bit that would hold him in thrall,
Plunges and bucks till the boy that's astride of him
    Goes to the ground with a terrible fall.

"Stop him there! Block him there! Drive him in carefully,
    Lead him about till he's quiet and cool.
Sound as a bell! though he's blown himself fearfully,
    Now let us pick up this poor little fool.

"Stunned? Oh, by Jove, I'm afraid it's a case with him;
    Ride for the doctor! keep bathing his head!
Send for a cart to go down to our place with him"—
    No use! One long sigh and the little chap's dead.

Only a jockey-boy, foul-mouthed and bad you see,
    Ignorant, heathenish, gone to his rest.
Parson or Presbyter, Pharisee, Sadducee,
    What did you do for him?—bad was the best.

Negroes and foreigners, all have a claim on you;
    Yearly you send your well-advertised hoard,
But the poor jockey-boy—shame on you, shame on you,
    "Feed ye My little ones"—what said the Lord?

Him ye held less than the outer barbarian,
    Left him to die in his ignorant sin;
Have you no principles, humanitarian?
    Have you no precept—"Go gather them in?"

Knew he God's name? In his brutal profanity
   That name was an oath—out of many but one.
What did he get from our famed Christianity?
   Where has his soul—if he had any—gone?

Fourteen years old, and what was he taught of it?
   What did he know of God's infinite Grace?
Draw the dark curtain of shame o'er the thought of it
   Draw the shroud over the jockey-boy's face.

ONLY A JOCKEY
Oil on canvas board 18in. × 14in. 1974

Been There Before

THERE came a stranger to Walgett town,
 To Walgett town when the sun was low,
And he carried a thirst that was worth a crown,
 Yet how to quench it he did not know;
But he thought he might take those yokels down,
The guileless yokels of Walgett town.

They made him a bet in a private bar,
 In a private bar when the talk was high,
And they bet him some pounds no matter how far
 He could pelt a stone, yet he could not shy
A stone right over the river so brown,
The Darling River at Walgett town.

He knew that the river from bank to bank
 Was fifty yards, and he smiled a smile
As he trundled down; but his hopes they sank,
 For there wasn't a stone within fifty mile;
For the saltbush plain and the open down
Produce no quarries in Walgett town.

The yokels laughed at his hopes o'erthrown,
 And he stood awhile like a man in a dream;
Then he out of his pocket he fetched a stone,
 And pelted it over the silent stream—
He'd been there before; he had wandered down
On a previous visit to Walgett town.

BEEN THERE BEFORE
Oil on canvas board 18in. × 14in. 1974

City of Dreadful Thirst

THE stranger came from Narromine and made his little joke;
"They say we folks in Narromine are narrow-minded folk;
But all the smartest men down here are puzzled to define
A kind of new phenomenon that came to Narromine.

"Last summer up in Narromine 'twas gettin' rather warm—
Two hundred in the water-bag, and lookin' like a storm—
We all were in the private bar, the coolest place in town,
When out across the stretch of plain a cloud came rollin' down.

"We don't respect the clouds up there, they fill us with disgust,
They mostly bring a Bogan shower—three raindrops and some dust;
But each man, simultaneous-like, to each man said, 'I think
That cloud suggests it's up to us to have another drink!'

"There's clouds of rain and clouds of dust—we'd heard of them
            before,
And sometimes in the daily press we read of 'clouds of war'.
But—if this ain't the Gospel truth I hope that I may burst—
That cloud that came to Narromine was just a cloud of thirst.

"It wasn't like a common cloud, 'twas more a sort of haze;
It settled down about the street, and stopped for days and days;
And not a drop of dew could fall, and not a sunbeam shine
To pierce that dismal sort of mist that hung on Narromine.

"Oh, Lord! we had a dreadful time beneath that cloud of thirst!
We all chucked-up our daily work and went upon the burst.
The very blacks about the town, that used to cadge for grub,
They made an organized attack and tried to loot the pub.

"We couldn't leave the private bar no matter how we tried;
Shearers and squatters, union-men and blacklegs side by side
Were drinkin' there and dursn't move, for each was sure, he said,
Before he'd get a half-a-mile the thirst would strike him dead!

"We drank until the drink gave out; we searched from room to room,
And round the pub, like drunken ghosts, went howling through
            the gloom.
The shearers found some kerosene and settled down again,
But all the squatter chaps and I, we staggered to the train.

"And once outside the cloud of thirst we felt as right as pie,
But while we stopped about the town we had to drink or die.
I hear today it's safe enough; I'm going back to work
Because they say the cloud of thirst has shifted on to Bourke.

CITY OF DREADFUL THIRST
Oil on hardboard 18in. × 14in. 1974

"But when you see those clouds about—like this one over here—
All white and frothy at the top, just like a pint of beer,
It's time to go and have a drink, for if that cloud should burst
You'd find the drink would all be gone, for that's a cloud of thirst!"

.   .   .   .   .   .

We stood the man from Narromine a pint of half-and-half;
He drank it off without a gasp in one tremendous quaff;
"I joined some friends last night," he said, "in what *they* called a
        spree;
But after Narromine 'twas just a holiday to me.

And now beyond the Western Range, where sunset skies are red,
And clouds of dust, and clouds of thirst, go drifting overhead,
The railway-train is taking back, along the Western Line,
That narrow-minded person on his road to Narromine.

THE TRAVELLING POST OFFICE
Oil on hardboard 35 x 45 cm 1976

Old Pardon, the Son of Reprieve

You never heard tell of the story?
  Well, now, I can hardly believe!
Never heard of the honour and glory
  Of Pardon, the son of Reprieve?
But maybe you're only a Johnnie
  And don't know a horse from a hoe?
Well, well, don't get angry, my sonny,
  But, really, a young un should know.

They bred him out back on the "Never",
  His mother was Mameluke breed.
To the front — and then stay there — was ever
  The root of the Mameluke creed.
He seemed to inherit their wiry
  Strong frames — and their pluck to receive —
As hard as a flint and as fiery
  Was Pardon, the son of Reprieve.

We ran him at many a meeting
  At crossing and gully and town,
And nothing could give him a beating —
  At least when our money was down.
For weight wouldn't stop him, nor distance,
  Nor odds, though the others were fast;
He'd race with a dogged persistence,
  And wear them all down at the last.

At the Turon the Yattendon filly
  Led by lengths at the mile-and-a-half,
And we all began to look silly,
  While her crowd were starting to laugh;
But the old horse came faster and faster,
  His pluck told its tale, and his strength,
He gained on her, caught her, and passed her,
  And won it, hands-down, by a length.

And then we swooped down on Menindie
  To run for the President's Cup;
Oh! that's a sweet township — a shindy
  To them is board, lodging, and sup.
Eye-openers they are, and their system
  Is never to suffer defeat;
It's "win, tie, or wrangle" — to best 'em
  You must lose 'em, or else it's "dead heat".

OLD PARDON, THE SON OF REPRIEVE I
Oil on hardboard 46 x 68 cm 1976

We strolled down the township and found 'em
  At drinking and gaming and play;
If sorrows they had, why they drowned 'em,
  And betting was soon under way.
Their horses were good uns and fit uns,
  There was plenty of cash in the town;
They backed their own horses like Britons,
  And, Lord! how *we* rattled it down!

With gladness we thought of the morrow,
  We counted our wages with glee,
A simile homely to borrow —
  "There was plenty of milk in our tea."
You see we were green; and we never
  Had even a thought of foul play,
Though we well might have known that the clever
  Division would "put us away".

Experience *docet*, they tell us,
  At least so I've frequently heard;
But, "dosing" or "stuffing", those fellows
  Were up to each move on the board:
They got to his stall — it is sinful
  To think what such villains will do —
And they gave him a regular skinful
  Of barley — green barley — to chew.

He munched it all night, and we found him
  Next morning as full as a hog —
The girths wouldn't nearly meet round him;
  He looked like an overfed frog.
We saw we were done like a dinner —
  The odds were a thousand to one
Against Pardon turning up winner,
  'Twas cruel to ask him to run.

We got to the course with our troubles,
  A crestfallen couple were we;
And we heard the "books" calling the doubles —
  A roar like the surf of the sea;
And over the tumult and louder
  Rang "Any price Pardon, I lay!"
Says Jimmy, "The children of Judah
  Are out on the warpath today."

OLD PARDON, THE SON OF REPRIEVE II
Oil on canvas board 41 x 51 cm 1976

Three miles in three heats: — Ah, my sonny,
  The horses in those days were stout,
They had to run well to win money;
  I don't see such horses about.
Your six-furlong vermin that scamper
  Half-a-mile with their feather-weight up,
They wouldn't earn much of their damper
  In a race like the President's Cup.

The first heat was soon set a-going;
  The Dancer went off to the front;
The Don on his quarters was showing,
  With Pardon right out of the hunt.
He rolled and he weltered and wallowed —
  You'd kick your hat faster, I'll bet;
They finished all bunched, and he followed
  All lathered and dripping with sweat.

But troubles came thicker upon us,
  For while we were rubbing him dry
The stewards came over to warn us:
  "We hear you are running a bye!
If Pardon don't spiel like tarnation
  And win the next heat — if he can —
He'll earn a disqualification;
  Just think over *that* now, my man!"

Our money all gone and our credit,
  Our horse couldn't gallop a yard;
And then people thought that *we* did it
  It really was terribly hard.
We were objects of mirth and derision
  To folks in the lawn and the stand,
And the yells of the clever division
  Of "Any price Pardon!" were grand.

We still had a chance for the money,
  Two heats still remained to be run:
If both fell to us — why, my sonny,
  The clever division were done.
And Pardon was better, we reckoned,
  His sickness was passing away,
So we went to the post for the second
  And principal heat of the day.

They're off and away with a rattle,
  Like dogs from the leashes let slip,
And right at the back of the battle
  He followed them under the whip.
They gained ten good lengths on him quickly
  He dropped right away from the pack;
I tell you it made me feel sickly
  To see the blue jacket fall back.

Our very last hope had departed —
  We thought the old fellow was done,
When all of a sudden he started
  To go like a shot from a gun.
His chances seemed slight to embolden
  Our hearts; but, with teeth firmly set,
We thought, "Now or never! The old un
  May reckon with some of 'em yet."

Then loud rose the war-cry from Pardon;
  He swept like the wind down the dip,
And over the rise by the garden
  The jockey was done with the whip.
The field was at sixes and sevens —
  The pace at the first had been fast —
And hope seemed to drop from the heavens,
  For Pardon was coming at last.

And how he did come! It was splendid;
  He gained on them yards every bound,
Stretching out like a greyhound extended,
  His girth laid right down on the ground.
A shimmer of silk in the cedars
  As into the running they wheeled,
And out flashed the whips on the leaders,
  For Pardon had collared the field.

Then right through the ruck he was sailing —
  I knew that the battle was won —
The son of Haphazard was failing,
  The Yattendon filly was done;
He cut down The Don and The Dancer,
  He raced clean away from the mare —
He's in front! Catch him now if you can, sir!
  And up went my hat in the air!

Then loud from the lawn and the garden
　　Rose offers of "Ten to one *on!*"
"Who'll bet on the field? I back Pardon!"
　　No use; all the money was gone.
He came for the third heat light-hearted,
　　A-jumping and dancing about;
The others were done ere they started
　　Crestfallen, and tired, and worn out.

He won it, and ran it much faster
　　Than even the first, I believe;
Oh, he was the daddy, the master,
　　Was Pardon, the son of Reprieve.
He showed 'em the method of travel —
　　The boy sat still as a stone —
They never could see him for gravel;
　　He came in hard-held, and alone.

　　　　　.　　　.　　　.

But he's old — and his eyes are grown hollow
　　Like me, with my thatch of the snow;
When he dies, then I hope I may follow,
　　And go where the racehorses go.
I don't want no harping nor singing —
　　Such things with my style don't agree;
Where the hoofs of the horses are ringing
　　There's music sufficient for me.

And surely the thoroughbred horses
　　Will rise up again and begin
Fresh races on far-away courses,
　　And p'raps they might let me slip in.
It would look rather well the race-card on
　　'Mongst Cherubs and Seraphs and things,
"Angel Harrison's black gelding Pardon,
　　Blue halo, white body and wings."

And if they have racing hereafter,
　　(And who is to say they will not?)
When the cheers and the shouting and laughter
　　Proclaim that the battle grows hot;
As they come down the racecourse a-steering,
　　He'll rush to the front, I believe;
And you'll hear the great multitude cheering
　　For Pardon, the son of Reprieve.

OLD PARDON, THE SON OF REPRIEVE III
Oil on hardboard 35 x 45 cm 1976

"Shouting" for a Camel

It was over at Coolgardie that a mining speculator,
    Who was going down the township just to make a bit o' chink,
Went off to hire a camel from a camel propagator,
    And the Afghan said he'd lend it if he'd stand the beast a drink.
Yes, the only price he asked him was to stand the beast a drink.
He was cheap, very cheap, as the dromedaries go.

So the mining speculator made the bargain, proudly thinking
    He had bested old Mahomet, he had done him in the eye.
Then he clambered on the camel, and the while the beast was
        drinking
    He explained with satisfaction to the miners standing by
That 'twas cheap, very cheap, as the dromedaries go.

But the camel kept on drinking and he filled his hold with water,
    And the more he had inside him yet the more he seemed to need;
For he drank it by the gallon, and his girths grew taut and tauter,
    And the miners muttered softly, "Yes he's very dry indeed!
But he's cheap, very cheap, as the dromedaries go."

So he drank up twenty buckets — it was weird to watch him suck it,
    (And the market price for water was per bucket half-a-crown)
Till the speculator stopped him, saying, "Not another bucket —
    If I give him any more there'll be a famine in the town.
Take him back to old Mahomet, and I'll tramp it through the
        town."
He was cheap, very cheap, as the speculators go.

There's a moral to this story — in your hat you ought to paste it —
    Be careful whom you shout for when a camel is about,
And there's plenty human camels who, before they'll see you
        waste it,
    Will drink up all you pay for if you're fool enough to shout;
If you chance to strike a camel when you're fool enough to shout,
You'll be cheap, very cheap, as the speculators go.

"SHOUTING" FOR A CAMEL
Oil on hardboard 35 x 45 cm 1976

Pioneers

THEY came of bold and roving stock that would not fixed abide;
They were the sons of field and flock since e'er they learnt to ride,
We may not hope to see such men in these degenerate years
As those explorers of the bush — the brave old pioneers.

'Twas they who rode the trackless bush in heat and storm and
        drought;
'Twas they who heard the master-word that called them farther
        out;
'Twas they who followed up the trail the mountain cattle made,
And pressed across the mighty range where now their bones are laid.

But now the times are dull and slow, the brave old days are dead
When hardy bushmen started out, and forced their way ahead
By tangled scrub and forests grim towards the unknown west,
And spied at last the promised land from off the range's crest.

O ye that sleep in lonely graves by distant ridge and plain,
We drink to you in silence now as Christmas comes again,
To you who fought the wilderness through rough unsettled years —
The founders of our nation's life, the brave old pioneers.

PIONEERS
Oil on hardboard 35 x 49 cm 1976

The Man Who Was Away

THE widow sought the lawyer's room with children three in tow,
She told the lawyer man her tale in tones of deepest woe.
She said, "My husband took to drink for pains in his inside,
And never drew a sober breath from then until he died.

"He never drew a sober breath, he died without a will,
And I must sell the bit of land the childer's mouths to fill.
There's some is grown and gone away, but some is childer yet,
And times is very bad indeed — a livin's hard to get.

"There's Min and Sis and little Chris, they stops at home with me,
And Sal has married Greenhide Bill that breaks for Bidgeree.
And Fred is drovin' Conroy's sheep along the Castlereagh
And Charley's shearin' down the Bland, and Peter is away."

The lawyer wrote the details down in ink of legal blue —
"There's Minnie, Susan, Christopher, they stop at home with you;
There's Sarah, Frederick, and Charles, I'll write to them today,
But what about the other son — the one who is away?

"You'll have to furnish his consent to sell the bit of land."
The widow shuffled in her seat, "Oh, don't you understand?
I thought a lawyer ought to know — I don't know what to say —
You'll have to do without him, boss, for Peter is away."

But here the little boy spoke up — said he, "We thought you knew;
He's done six months in Goulburn gaol — he's got six more to do."
Thus in one comprehensive flash he made it clear as day,
The mystery of Peter's life — the man who was away.

THE MAN WHO WAS AWAY
Oil on hardboard 35 x 45 cm 1976

The Open Steeple-chase

I HAD ridden over hurdles up the country once or twice,
By the side of Snowy River with a horse they called "The Ace".
And we brought him down to Sydney, and our rider, Jimmy Rice,
Got a fall and broke his shoulder, so they nabbed me in a trice —
Me, that never wore the colours, for the Open Steeplechase.

"Make the running," said the trainer, "it's your only chance
　　　　whatever,
Make it hot from start to finish, for the old black horse can stay,
And just think of how they'll take it, when they hear on Snowy
　　　　River
That the country boy was plucky, and the country horse was
　　　　clever.
You must ride for old Monaro and the mountain boys today."

"Are you ready?" said the starter, as we held the horses back.
All ablazing with impatience, with excitement all aglow;
Before us like a ribbon stretched the steeplechasing track,
And the sun-rays glistened brightly on the chestnut and the black
As the starter's words came slowly, "Are — you — ready? Go!"

Well I scarcely knew we'd started, I was stupid-like with wonder
Till the field closed up beside me and a jump appeared ahead.
And we flew it like a hurdle, not a baulk and not a blunder,
As we charged it all together, and it fairly whistled under,
And then some were pulled behind me and a few shot out and led.

So we ran for half the distance, and I'm making no pretences
When I tell you I was feeling very nervous-like and queer,
For those jockeys rode like demons; you would think they'd lost
　　　　their senses
If you saw them rush their horses at those rasping five-foot fences —
And in place of making running I was falling to the rear.

Till a chap came racing past me on a horse they called "The
　　　　Quiver",
And said he, "My country joker, are you going to give it best?
Are you frightened of the fences? does their stoutness make you
　　　　shiver?
Have they come to breeding cowards by the side of Snowy River?
Are there riders on Monaro? — " but I never heard the rest.

THE OPEN STEEPLECHASE I
Oil on hardboard 35 x 45 cm 1976

For I drove The Ace and sent him just as fast as he could pace it
At the big black line of timber stretching fair across the track,
And he shot beside The Quiver. "Now," said I, "my boy, we'll
     race it.
You can come with Snowy River if you're only game to face it,
Let us mend the pace a little and we'll see who cries a crack."

So we raced away together, and we left the others standing,
And the people cheered and shouted as we settled down to ride,
And we clung beside The Quiver. At his taking off and landing
I could see his scarlet nostril and his mighty ribs expanding,
And The Ace stretched out in earnest, and we held him stride
     for stride.

But the pace was so terrific that they soon ran out their tether —
They were rolling in their gallop, they were fairly blown and
     beat —
But they both were game as pebbles — neither one would show the
     feather.
And we rushed them at the fences, and they cleared them both
     together,
Nearly every time they clouted, but they somehow kept their feet.

Then the last jump rose before us, and they faced it game as
     ever —
We were both at spur and whipcord, fetching blood at every
     bound —
And above the people's cheering and the cries of "Ace" and "Quiver',
I could hear the trainer shouting, "One more run for Snowy River."
Then we struck the jump together and came smashing to the
     ground.

Well, The Quiver ran to blazes, but The Ace stood still and
     waited,
Stood and waited like a statue while I scrambled on his back.
There was no one next or near me for the field was fairly slated,
So I cantered home a winner with my shoulder dislocated,
While the man who rode The Quiver followed limping down the
     track.

And he shook my hand and told me that in all his days he never
Met a man who rode more gamely, and our last set-to was prime.
Then we wired them on Monaro how we chanced to beat The
     Quiver,
And they sent us back an answer, "Good old sort from Snowy
     River:
Send us word each race you start in and we'll back you every
     time."

THE OPEN STEEPLECHASE II
Oil on hardboard 35 x 45 cm 1976

The Last Trump

"You led the trump," the old man said
  With fury in his eye,
"And yet you hope my girl to wed!
Young man! your hopes of love are fled,
  'Twere better she should die!

"My sweet young daughter sitting there,
  So innocent and plump!
You don't suppose that she would care
To wed an outlawed man who'd dare
  To lead the thirteenth trump!

"If you had drawn their leading spade
  It meant a certain win!
But no! By Pembroke's mighty shade
The thirteenth trump you went and played
  And let their diamonds in!

"My girl, return at my command
  His presents in a lump!
Return his ring! For, understand,
No man is fit to hold your hand
  Who leads a thirteenth trump!

"But hold! Give every man his due
  And every dog his day.
Speak up and say what made you do
This dreadful thing — that is, if you
  Have anything to say!"

He spoke. "I meant at first," said he,
  "To give their spades a bump,
Or lead the hearts; but then you see
I thought against us there might be,
  Perhaps, a fourteenth trump!"

              ·   ·   ·

They buried him at dawn of day
  Beside a ruined stump:
And there he sleeps the hours away
And waits for Gabriel to play
  The last — the fourteenth trump.

THE LAST TRUMP
Oil on hardboard 39 x 45 cm 1976

The Flying Gang

I SERVED my time, in the days gone by,
  In the railway's clash and clang,
And I worked my way to the end, and I
  Was the head of the "Flying Gang".
'Twas a chosen band that was kept at hand
  In case of an urgent need;
Was it south or north, we were started forth
  And away at our utmost speed.
If word reached town that a bridge was down,
  The imperious summons rang —
"Come out with the pilot engine sharp,
  And away with the flying gang."

Then a piercing scream and a rush of steam
  As the engine moved ahead;
With measured beat by the slum and street
  Of the busy town we fled,
By the uplands bright and the homesteads white,
  With the rush of the western gale —
And the pilot swayed with the pace we made
  As she rocked on the ringing rail.
And the country children clapped their hands
  As the engine's echoes rang.
But their elders said: "There is work ahead
  When they send for the flying gang."

Then across the miles of the saltbush plain
  That gleamed with the morning dew,
Where the grasses waved like the ripening grain
  The pilot engine flew —
A fiery rush in the open bush
  Where the grade marks seemed to fly,
And the order sped on the wires ahead,
  The pilot *must* go by.
The Governor's special must stand aside,
  And the fast express go hang;
Let your orders be that the line is free
  For the boys of the flying gang.

THE FLYING GANG
Oil on hardboard 35 x 45 cm 1976

How M'Ginnis Went Missing

LET us cease our idle chatter,
  Let the tears bedew our cheek,
For a man from Tallangatta
  Has been missing for a week.

Where the roaring flooded Murray
  Covered all the lower land,
There he started in a hurry,
  With a bottle in his hand.

And his fate is hid for ever,
  But the public seem to think
That he slumbered by the river,
  'Neath the influence of drink.

And they scarcely seem to wonder
  That the river, wide and deep,
Never woke him with its thunder,
  Never stirred him in his sleep.

As the crashing logs came sweeping
  And their tumult filled the air,
Then M'Ginnis murmured, sleeping,
  "'Tis a wake in ould Kildare."

So the river rose and found him
  Sleeping softly by the stream.
And the cruel waters drowned him
  Ere he wakened from his dream.

And the blossom-tufted wattle,
  Blooming brightly on the lea,
Saw M'Ginnis and the bottle
  Going drifting out to sea.

HOW M'GINNIS WENT MISSING
Oil on hardboard 40 x 30 cm 1976

Last Week

Oh, the new chum went to the backblock run,
But he should have gone there last week.
He tramped ten miles with a loaded gun,
But of turkey or duck saw never a one,
For he should have been there last week,
  They said,
There were flocks of 'em there last week.

He wended his way to a waterfall,
And he should have gone there last week.
He carried a camera, legs and all,
But the day was hot and the stream was small,
For he should have gone there last week,
  They said,
They drowned a man there last week.

He went for a drive, and he made a start,
Which should have been made last week,
For the old horse died of a broken heart;
So he footed it home and he dragged the cart —
But the horse was all right last week,
  They said,
He trotted a match last week.

So he asked the bushies who came from afar
To visit the town last week
If they'd dine with him, and they said "Hurrah!"
But there wasn't a drop in the whisky jar —
You should have been here last week,
  He said,
I drank it all up last week!

LAST WEEK
Oil on hardboard 35 x 45 cm 1976

Saltbush Bill's Gamecock

'Twas Saltbush Bill, with his travelling sheep, was making his way
    to town;
He crossed them over the Hard Times Run, and he came to the
    Take 'Em Down;
He counted through at the boundary gate, and camped at the
    drafting yard:
For Stingy Smith, of the Hard Times Run, had hunted him rather
    hard.
He bore no malice to Stingy Smith — 'twas simply the hand of Fate
That caused his waggon to swerve aside and shatter old Stingy's gate;
And being only the hand of Fate, it follows, without a doubt,
It wasn't the fault of Saltbush Bill that Stingy's sheep got out.
So Saltbush Bill, with an easy heart, prepared for what might befall,
Commenced his stages on Take 'Em Down, the station of Rooster
    Hall.

'Tis strange how often the men out back will take to some curious
    craft,
Some ruling passion to keep their thoughts away from the overdraft;
And Rooster Hall, of the Take 'Em Down, was widely known to
    fame
As breeder of champion fighting cocks — his *forte* was the British
    Game.

The passing stranger within his gates that camped with old Rooster
    Hall
Was forced to talk about fowls all night, or else not talk at all.
Though droughts should come, and though sheep should die, his
    fowls were his sole delight;
He left his shed in the flood of work to watch two gamecocks fight.
He held in scorn the Australian Game, that long-legged child of sin;
In a desperate fight, with the steel-tipped spurs, the British game
    must win!
The Australian bird was a mongrel bird, with a touch of the
    jungle cock;
The want of breeding must find him out, when facing the English
    stock;
For British breeding, and British pluck, must triumph it over all —
And that was the root of the simple creed that governed old
    Rooster Hall.

.   .   .   .   .   .

SALTBUSH BILL'S GAMECOCK I
Oil on hardboard 40 x 50 cm 1976

'Twas Saltbush Bill to the station rode ahead of his travelling
    sheep,
And sent a message to Rooster Hall that wakened him out of his
    sleep —
A crafty message that fetched him out, and hurried him as he
    came —
"A drover has an Australian bird to match with your British Game."
'Twas done, and done in half a trice; a five-pound note a side;
Old Rooster Hall, with his champion bird, and the drover's bird
    untried.

"Steel spurs, of course?" said old Rooster Hall; "you'll need 'em
    without a doubt!"
"You stick the spurs on your bird!" said Bill, "but mine fights best
    without."
"Fights best without?" said old Rooster Hall; "he can't fight best
    unspurred!
You must be crazy!" But Saltbush Bill said, "Wait till you see my
    bird!"
So Rooster Hall to his fowl-yard went, and quickly back he came,
Bearing a clipt and a shaven cock, the pride of his English Game;
With an eye as fierce as an eaglehawk, and a crow like a trumpet
    call,
He strutted about on the garden walk, and cackled at Rooster
    Hall.
Then Rooster Hall sent off a boy with a word to his cronies two,
McCrae (the boss of the Black Police) and Father Donahoo.

Full many a cockfight old McCrae had held in his empty Court,
With Father D. as the picker-up — a regular all-round Sport!
They got the message of Rooster Hall, and down to his run they
    came,
Prepared to scoff at the drover's bird, and to bet on the English
    Game;
They hied them off to the drover's camp, while Saltbush rode
    before —
Old Rooster Hall was a blithsome man, when he thought of the
    treat in store.
They reached the camp, where the drover's cook, with countenance
    all serene,
Was boiling beef in an iron pot, but never a fowl was seen.

SALTBUSH BILL'S GAMECOCK II
Oil on hardboard 35 x 45 cm 1976

"Take off the beef from the fire," said Bill, "and wait till you see the fight;
There's something fresh for the bill-of-fare — there's game-fowl stew tonight!
For Mister Hall has a fighting cock, all feathered and clipped and spurred;
And he's fetched him here, for a bit of sport, to fight our Australian bird.
I've made a match that our pet will win, though he's hardly a fighting cock,
But he's game enough, and it's many a mile that he's tramped with the travelling stock."
The cook he banged on a saucepan lid; and, soon as the sound was heard,
Under the dray, in the shallow hid, a something moved and stirred:
A great tame emu strutted out. Said Saltbush, "Here's our bird!"
But Rooster Hall, and his cronies two, drove home without a word.

The passing stranger within his gates that camps with old Rooster Hall
Must talk about something else than fowls, if he wishes to talk at all.
For the record lies in the local Court, and filed in its deepest vault,
That Peter Hall, of the Take 'Em Down, was tried for a fierce assault
On a stranger man, who, in all good faith, and prompted by what he heard,
Had asked old Hall if a British Game could beat an Australian bird;
And Old McCrae, who was on the Bench as soon as the case was tried,
Remarked, "Discharged with a clean discharge — the assault was justified!"

SALTBUSH BILL'S GAMECOCK III
Oil on hardboard 40 x 49 cm 1976

A Bushman's Song

I'M travelling down the Castlereagh, and I'm a station-hand,
I'm handy with the ropin' pole, I'm handy with the brand,
And I can ride a rowdy colt, or swing the axe all day,
But there's no demand for a station-hand along the Castlereagh.

So it's shift, boys, shift, for there isn't the slightest doubt
That we've got to make a shift to the stations further out,
With the pack-horse runnin' after, for he follows like a dog,
We must strike across the country at the old jig-jog.

This old black horse I'm riding — if you'll notice what's his brand,
He wears the crooked R, you see — none better in the land.
He takes a lot of beatin', and the other day we tried,
For a bit of a joke, with a racing bloke, for twenty pound a side.

It was shift, boys, shift, for there wasn't the slightest doubt
That I had to make him shift, for the money was nearly out,
But he cantered home a winner, with the other one at the flog —
He's a red-hot sort to pick up with his old jig-jog.

I asked a cove for shearin' once along the Marthaguy:
"We shear non-union here," says he. "I call it scab," says I.
I looked along the shearin' floor before I turned to go —
There were eight or ten dashed Chinamen a-shearin' in a row.

It was shift, boys, shift, for there wasn't the slightest doubt
It was time to make a shift with the leprosy about.
So I saddled up my horses, and I whistled to my dog,
And I left his scabby station at the old jig-jog.

I went to Illawarra, where my brother's got a farm;
He has to ask his landlord's leave before he lifts his arm:
The landlord owns the country-side — man, woman, dog, and cat,
They haven't the cheek to dare to speak without they touch their hat.

It was shift, boys, shift, for there wasn't the slightest doubt
Their little landlord god and I would soon have fallen out,
Was I to touch my hat to him? — was I his bloomin' dog?
So I makes for up the country at the old jig-jog.

A BUSHMAN'S SONG
Oil on hardboard 35 x 45 cm 1976

But it's time that I was movin', I've a mighty way to go
Till I drink artesian water from a thousand feet below;
Till I meet the overlanders with the cattle comin' down —
And I'll work a while till I make a pile, then have a spree in town.

So it's shift, boys, shift, for there isn't the slightest doubt
We've got to make a shift to the stations further out:
The pack-horse runs behind us, for he follows like a dog,
And we cross a lot of country at the old jig-jog.

Father Riley's Horse

'TWAS the horse thief, Andy Regan, that was hunted like a dog
  By the troopers of the Upper Murray side;
They had searched in every gully, they had looked in every log
  But never sight or track of him they spied,
Till the priest at Kiley's Crossing heard a knocking very late
  And a whisper "Father Riley — come across!"
So his Reverence, in pyjamas, trotted softly to the gate
  And admitted Andy Regan — and a horse!

"Now, it's listen, Father Riley, to the words I've got to say,
  For it's close upon the death I am tonight.
With the troopers hard behind me I've been hiding all the day
  In the gullies keeping close and out of sight.
But they're watching all the ranges till there's not a bird could fly,
  And I'm fairly worn to pieces with the strife,
So I'm taking no more trouble, but I'm going home to die,
  'Tis the only way I see to save my life.

"Yes, I'm making home to mother's, and I'll die o' Tuesday next
  An' buried on the Thursday — and, of course,
I'm prepared to do my penance; but with one thing I'm perplexed
  And it's — Father, it's this jewel of a horse!
He was never bought nor paid for, and there's not a man can
    swear
  To his owner or his breeder, but I know
That his sire was by Pedantic from the Old Pretender mare,
  And his dam was close related to The Roe.

"And there's nothing in the district that can race him for a step —
  He could canter while they're going at their top:
He's the king of all the leppers that was ever seen to lep;
  A five-foot fence — he'd clear it in a hop!
So I'll leave him with you, Father, till the dead shall rise again,
  'Tis yourself that knows a good un; and, of course,
You can say he's got by Moonlight out of Paddy Murphy's plain
  If you're ever asked the breeding of the horse!

"But it's getting on to daylight, and it's time to say good-bye,
  For the stars above the East are growing pale.
And I'm making home to mother — and it's hard for me to die!
  But it's harder still, is keeping out of gaol!
You can ride the old horse over to my grave across the dip,
  Where the wattle-bloom is waving overhead.
Sure he'll jump them fences easy — you must never raise the whip
  Or he'll rush 'em! — now, good-bye!" and he had fled!

So they buried Andy Regan, and they buried him to rights,
　　In the graveyard at the back of Kiley's Hill;
There were five-and-twenty mourners who had five-and-twenty fights
　　Till the very boldest fighters had their fill.
There were fifty horses racing from the graveyard to the pub.
　　And the riders flogged each other all the while —
And the lashins of the liquor! And the lavins of the grub!
　　Oh, poor Andy went to rest in proper style.

Then the races came to Kiley's — with a steeple chase and all,
　　For the folk were mostly Irish round about,
And it takes an Irish rider to be fearless of a fall;
　　They were training morning in and morning out.
But they never started training till the sun was on the course,
　　For a superstitious story kept 'em back.
That the ghost of Andy Regan on a slashing chestnut horse
　　Had been training by the starlight on the track.

And they read the nominations for the races with surprise
　　And amusement at the Father's little joke,
For a novice had been entered for the steeplechasing prize,
　　And they found that it was Father Riley's moke!
He was neat enough to gallop, he was strong enough to stay!
　　But his owner's views of training were immense,
For the Reverend Father Riley used to ride him every day,
　　And he never saw a hurdle nor a fence.

And the priest would join the laughter, "Oh," said he, "I put him in,
　　For there's five-and-twenty sovereigns to be won;
And the poor would find it useful if the chestnut chanced to win.
　　As he'll maybe do when all is said and done!"
He had called him Faugh-a-ballagh (which is French for 'Clear
　　　the course'),
　　And his colours were a vivid shade of green:
All the Dooleys and O'Donnells were on Father Riley's horse,
　　While the Orangeman were backing Mandarin!

It was Hogan, the dog-poisoner — aged man and very wise,
　　Who was camping in the racecourse with his swag,
And who ventured the opinion, to the township's great surprise,
　　That the race would go to Father Riley's nag.
"You can talk about your riders — and the horse has not been
　　　schooled,
　　And the fences is terrific, and the rest!
When the field is fairly going, then ye'll see ye've all been fooled.
　　And the chestnut horse will battle with the best.

FATHER RILEY'S HORSE I
Oil on hardboard 40 x 50 cm 1976

"For there's some has got condition, and they think the race is
        sure,
    And the chestnut horse will fall beneath the weight;
But the hopes of all the helpless, and the prayers of all the poor,
    Will be running by his side to keep him straight.
And it's what the need of schoolin' or of workin' on the track,
    Whin the Saints are there to guide him round the course!
I've prayed him over every fence — I've prayed him out and back!
    And I'll bet my cash on Father Riley's horse!"

       .   .   .   .   .

Oh, the steeple was a caution! They went tearin' round and round,
    And the fences rang and rattled where they struck.
There was some that cleared the water — there was more fell in and
        drowned —
    Some blamed the men and others blamed the luck!
But the whips were flying freely when the field came into view
    For the finish down the long green stretch of course,
And in front of all the flyers, jumpin' like a kangaroo,
    Came the rank outsider — Father Riley's horse!

Oh, the shouting and the cheering as he rattled past the post!
    For he left the others standing, in the straight;
And the rider — well, they reckoned it was Andy Regan's ghost,
    And it beat 'em how a ghost would draw the weight!
But he weighed in, nine stone seven; then he laughed and dis-
        appeared,
    Like a Banshee (which is Spanish for an elf),
And old Hogan muttered sagely, "If it wasn't for the beard
    They'd be thinking it was Andy Regan's self!"

And the poor at Kiley's Crossing drank the health at Christmastide
    Of the chestnut and his rider dressed in green.
There was never such a rider, not since Andy Regan died,
    And they wondered who on earth he could have been,
But they settled it amongst 'em, for the story got about,
    'Mongst the bushmen and the people on the course,
That the Devil had been ordered to let Andy Regan out
    For the steeplechase on Father Riley's horse!

FATHER RILEY'S HORSE II
Oil on hardboard 35 x 45 cm 1976

Riders in the Stand

THERE'S some that ride the Robbo style, and bump at every stride;
While others sit a long way back, to get a longer ride.
There's some that ride as sailors do, with legs, and arms, and teeth;
And some ride on the horse's neck, and some ride underneath.

But all the finest horsemen out — the men to Beat the Band —
You'll find amongst the crowd that ride their races in the Stand.
They'll say "He had the race in hand, and lost it in the straight."
They'll show how Godby came too soon, and Barden came too late.

They'll say Chevalley lost his nerve, and Regan lost his head;
They'll tell how one was "livened up" and something else was
    "dead" —
In fact, the race was never run on sea, or sky, or land,
But what you'd get it better done by riders in the Stand.

The rule holds good in everything in life's uncertain fight;
You'll find the winner can't go wrong, the loser can't go right.
You ride a slashing race, and lose — by one and all you're banned!
Ride like a bag of flour, and win — they'll cheer you in the Stand.

RIDERS IN THE STAND
Oil on hardboard 35 x 45 cm 1976

Bottle-O!

I AIN'T the kind of bloke as takes to any steady job;
　　I drives me bottle cart around the town;
A bloke what keeps 'is eyes about can always make a bob —
　　I couldn't bear to graft for every brown.
There's lots of handy things about in everybody's yard,
　　There's cocks and hens a-runnin' to an' fro,
And little dogs what comes and barks — we take 'em off their guard
　　And we puts 'em with the Empty Bottle-O!

Chorus —

So it's any "Empty bottles! Any empty bottle-O!"
You can hear us round for half a mile or so.
　　And you'll see the women rushing
　　To take in the Monday's washing
When they 'ear us crying, "Empty Bottle-O!"

I'm driving down by Wexford-street and up a winder goes,
　　A girl sticks out 'er 'ead and looks at me,
An all-right tart with ginger 'air, and freckles on 'er nose;
　　I stops the cart and walks across to see.
"There ain't no bottles 'ere," says she, "since father took the pledge,"
　　"No bottles 'ere," says I, "I'd like to know
What right 'ave you to stick your 'ead outside the winder ledge,
　　If you 'aven't got no Empty Bottle-O!"

I sometimes gives the 'orse a spell, and then the push and me
　　We takes a little trip to Chowder Bay.
Oh! ain't it nice the 'ole day long a-gazin' at the sea
　　And a-hidin' of the tanglefoot away.
But when the booze gits 'old of us, and fellows starts to "scrap",
　　There's some what likes blue-metal for to throw:
But as for me, I always says for layin' out a "trap"
　　There's nothing like an Empty Bottle-O!

BOTTLE-O!
Oil on hardboard 35 x 45 cm 1976

Story of Mongrel Grey

THIS is the story the stockman told
  On the cattle-camp, when the stars were bright;
The moon rose up like a globe of gold
  And flooded the plain with her mellow light.
    We watched the cattle till dawn of day
    And he told me the story of Mongrel Grey.

He was a knock-about station hack,
  Spurred and walloped, and banged and beat;
Ridden all day with a sore on his back,
  Left all night with nothing to eat.
    That was a matter of everyday
    Normal occurrence with Mongrel Grey.

We might have sold him, but someone heard
  He was bred out back on a flooded run,
Where he learnt to swim like a waterbird;
  Midnight or midday were all as one —
    In the flooded ground he would find his way;
    Nothing could puzzle old Mongrel Grey.

'Tis a trick, no doubt, that some horses learn;
  When the floods are out they will splash along
In girth-deep water, and twist and turn
  From hidden channel and billabong,
    Never mistaking the road to go;
    For a man may guess — but the horses *know*.

I was camping out with my youngest son —
  Bit of a nipper, just learnt to speak —
In an empty hut on the lower run,
  Shooting and fishing in Conroy's Creek.
    The youngster toddled about all day
    And there with our horses was Mongrel Grey.

All of a sudden a flood came down,
  At first a freshet of mountain rain,
Roaring and eddying, rank and brown,
  Over the flats and across the plain.
    Rising and rising — at fall of night
    Nothing but water appeared in sight!

STORY OF MONGREL GREY
Oil on hardboard 35 x 45 cm 1976

'Tis a nasty place when the floods are out,
  Even in daylight; for all around
Channels and billabongs twist about,
  Stretching for miles in the flooded ground.
      And to move seemed a hopeless thing to try
      In the dark with the storm-water racing by.

I had to risk it. I heard a roar
  As the wind swept down and the driving rain;
And the water rose till it reached the floor
  Of our highest room; and 'twas very plain —
      The way the torrent was sweeping down —
      We must make for the highlands at once, or drown.

Off to the stable I splashed, and found
  The horses shaking with cold and fright;
I led them down to the lower ground,
  But never a yard would they swim that night!
      They reared and snorted and turned away,
      And none would face it but Mongrel Grey.

I bound the child on the horse's back,
  And we started off, with a prayer to heaven,
Through the rain and the wind and the pitchy black
  For I knew that the instinct God has given
      To prompt His creatures by night and day
      Would guide the footsteps of Mongrel Grey.

He struck deep water at once and swam —
  I swam beside him and held his mane —
Till we touched the bank of the broken dam
  In shallow water; then off again,
      Swimming in darkness across the flood,
      Rank with the smell of the drifting mud.

He turned and twisted across and back,
  Choosing the places to wade or swim,
Picking the safest and shortest track —
  The blackest darkness was clear to him.
      Did he strike the crossing by sight or smell?
      The Lord that held him alone could tell!

He dodged the timber whene'er he could,
  But timber brought us to grief at last;
I was partly stunned by a log of wood
  That struck my head as it drifted past;
    Then lost my grip of the brave old grey,
    And in half a second he swept away.

I reached a tree, where I had to stay,
  And did a perish for two day's hard;
And lived on water — but Mongrel Grey,
  He walked right into the homestead yard
    At dawn next morning, and grazed around,
    With the child strapped on to him safe and sound.

We keep him now for the wife to ride,
  Nothing too good for him now, of course;
Never a whip on his fat old hide,
  For she owes the child to that brave grey horse.
    And not Old Tyson himself could pay
    The purchase money of Mongrel Grey.

A Mountain Station

I BOUGHT a run a while ago
  On country rough and ridgy,
Where wallaroos and wombats grow —
  The Upper Murrumbidgee.
The grass is rather scant, it's true,
  But this a fair exchange is,
The sheep can see a lovely view
  By climbing up the ranges.

And She-oak Flat's the station's name,
  I'm not surprised at that, sirs:
The oaks were there before I came,
  And I supplied the flat, sirs.
A man would wonder how it's done,
  The stock so soon decreases —
They sometimes tumble off the run
  And break themselves to pieces.

I've tried to make expenses meet,
  But wasted all my labours;
The sheep the dingoes didn't eat
  Were stolen by the neighbours.
They stole my pears — my native pears —
  Those thrice-convicted felons,
And ravished from me unawares
  My crop of paddy-melons.

And sometimes under sunny skies,
  Without an explanation,
The Murrumbidgee used to rise
  And overflow the station.
But this was caused (as now I know)
  When summer sunshine glowing
Had melted all Kiandra's snow
  And set the river going.

Then in the news, perhaps, you read:
  "Stock Passings. Puckawidgee,
Fat cattle: Seven hundred head
  Swept down the Murrumbidgee;
Their destination's quite obscure,
  But, somehow, there's a notion,
Unless the river falls, they're sure
  To reach the Southern Ocean."

A MOUNTAIN STATION I
Oil on hardboard 35 x 45 cm 1976

So after that I'll give it best;
   No more with Fate I'll battle.
I'll let the river take the rest,
   For those were all my cattle.
And with one comprehensive curse
   I close my brief narration,
And advertise it in my verse —
   "For Sale! A Mountain Station."

A MOUNTAIN STATION II
Oil on hardboard 35 x 45 cm 1976

Jim Carew

Born of a thoroughbred English race,
  Well proportioned and closely knit,
Neat, slim figure and handsome face,
  Always ready and always fit,
Hardy and wiry of limb and thew,
That was the ne'er-do-well Jim Carew.

One of the sons of the good old land —
  Many a year since his like was known;
Never a game but he took command,
  Never a sport but he held his own;
Gained at his college a triple blue —
Good as they make them was Jim Carew.

Came to grief — was it card or horse?
  Nobody asked and nobody cared;
Ship him away to the bush of course,
  Ne'er-do-well fellows are easily spared;
Only of women a sorrowing few
Wept at parting from Jim Carew.

Gentleman Jim on the cattle-camp
  Sitting his horse with an easy grace;
But the reckless living has left its stamp
  In the deep drawn lines of that handsome face,
And the harder look in those eyes of blue:
Prompt at a quarrel is Jim Carew.

Billy the Lasher was out for gore —
  Twelve-stone navvy with chest of hair —
When he opened out with a hungry roar
  On a ten-stone man, it was hardly fair;
But his wife was wise if his face she knew
By the time you were done with him, Jim Carew.

Gentleman Jim in the stockmen's hut
  Works with them, toils with them, side by side;
As to his past — well, his lips are shut.
  "Gentleman once," say his mates with pride,
And the wildest Cornstalk can ne'er outdo
In feats of recklessness Jim Carew.

JIM CAREW
Oil on hardboard 35 x 45 cm 1976

What should he live for? A dull despair!
    Drink is his master and drags him down,
Water of Lethe that drowns all care.
    Gentleman Jim has a lot to drown,
And he reigns as king with a drunken crew,
Sinking to misery, Jim Carew.

Such is the end of the ner'er-do-well —
    Jimmy the Boozer, all down at heel;
But he straightens up when he's asked to tell
    His name and race, and a flash of steel
Still lightens up in those eyes of blue —
"I am, or — no, I *was* — Jim Carew."

The Travelling Post Office

THE roving breezes come and go, the reed-beds sweep and sway,
The sleepy river murmurs low, and loiters on its way,
It is the land of lots o' time along the Castlereagh.

.   .   .   .   .

The old man's son had left the farm, he found it dull and slow,
He drifted to the great North-west, where all the rovers go.
"He's gone so long," the old man said; "he's dropped right out
    of mind,
But if you'd write a line to him I'd take it very kind;
He's shearing here and fencing there, a kind of waif and stray —
He's droving now with Conroy's sheep along the Castlereagh.

"The sheep are travelling for the grass, and travelling very slow;
They may be at Mundooran now, or past the Overflow,
Or tramping down the black-soil flats across by Waddiwong
But all those little country towns would send the letter wrong.
The mailman, if he's extra tired, would pass them in his sleep;
It's safest to address the note to 'Care of Conroy's sheep',
For five and twenty thousand head can scarcely go astray,
You write to 'Care of Conroy's sheep along the Castlereagh'."

.   .   .   .   .

By rock and ridge and riverside the western mail has gone
Across the great Blue Mountain Range to take that letter on.
A moment on the topmost grade, while open fire-doors glare,
She pauses like a living thing to breathe the mountain air,
Then launches down the other side across the plains away
To bear that note to "Conroy's sheep along the Castlereagh".

And now by coach and mailman's bag it goes from town to town,
And Conroy's Gap and Conroy's Creek have marked it "Further
    down".
Beneath a sky of deepest blue, where never cloud abides,
A speck upon the waste of plain the lonely mailman rides.
Where fierce hot winds have set the pine and myall boughs
    asweep
He hails the shearers passing by for news of Conroy's sheep.
By big lagoons where wildfowl play and crested pigeons flock,
By camp-fires where the drovers ride around their restless stock,
And past the teamster toiling down to fetch the wool away
My letter chases Conroy's sheep along the Castlereagh.